HAUNTED
HOUSES
GHOSTS
&demons

HAUNTED HOUSES HOUSES GHOSTS & demons

ROBERTS LIARDON

Banner Publishing

HAUNTED HOUSES, GHOSTS & DEMONS:
What You Can Do About Them

Roberts Liardon Ministries
P.O. Box 2989
Sarasota, FL 34230
E-mail: info1@robertsliardon.org
www.RobertsLiardon.com

ISBN: 978-1-62911-217-6
eBook ISBN: 978-1-62911-218-3
Printed in the United States of America
© 1998, 2014 by Roberts Liardon

Banner Publishing
1030 Hunt Valley Circle
New Kensington, PA 15068

1 2 3 4 5 6 7 8 9 10 11 🅱 20 19 18 17 16 15 14

CONTENTS

Introduction 7

1. Demons on the Rampage 9

2. The Fall from Glory 23

3. A Habitation of Demons 42

4. Following Jesus into Battle 52

5. The Gates of Hell Will Not Prevail 70

6. Seven Steps to Demon Possession 79

7. Moving Forward in the Power of God 109

About the Author 123

INTRODUCTION

We are living in a time when supernatural phenomena are everywhere. Psychic hotlines are advertised on television, movies explore the unusual extrasensory perception many people experience, and television programs have turned the imagination of a generation toward aliens from other planets. We seem to be obsessed with angels and spirit beings. Bookstores, movies, television shows, and magazines are filled with stories of people who claim to have encountered angels, spirits, and even creatures from other worlds.

All this begs some questions: Is all supernatural experience good? Is it all from God? And if not, how do we know what is God and what is not? (Who else could it be?) How do we know what is real and what is counterfeit? How do we know what is good and what is bad?

The Bible answers these questions very clearly, and through the years, I have gained tremendous insight into the supernatural that I will share with you. My experience of going to heaven as a young boy, where I talked with Jesus face-to-face, as well as my many years of ministry, have made me very familiar with what goes on in the spirit realm. However, most of what I am going to share with you is from the Bible, because the Bible is the only book that truly explains these things.

If you are having or have had supernatural experiences, you need to read this book! I promise you will have a true picture of what you're dealing with by the time you've finished reading, and any fears you have will be laid to rest. You can—and will—have peace in your life!

CHAPTER 1

DEMONS ON THE RAMPAGE

Along a dark and lonely railroad track in a small North Carolina town, five students from a nearby college stand and wait for a ghost to appear. They will not be disappointed.

It's approaching midnight when someone whispers excitedly, "Look! Do you see it?"

"Yes," the others answer in unison. "It's coming this way!"

Sure enough, about one hundred yards down the track, to the west, a faint glow has appeared on the tracks. It is not an approaching train but seems to be someone walking toward them. Someone swinging a kerosene lantern. The closer it gets, the brighter the light becomes and the more definite the movement. Some of the students think they see a human form behind the light—or at least the shape of an arm holding the lantern. It's coming closer and closer, and then it's gone!

The students are only mildly disappointed. They believe they have been in the presence of a ghost. For some of them, an appetite for the supernatural has been whetted. According to legend, the light that appears along this isolated stretch of railroad has to do with a brakeman who died here more than one hundred years ago. There was a ghastly accident, and the poor man was decapitated.

Since then, he comes every night to walk along the railroad tracks near where he was killed.

That is the explanation for this strange light. But what is it really?

FRIEND OR FOE?

In Pennsylvania, a young couple is ecstatic when they move into their new home. It is an old house that needs quite a bit of work, but it's in a terrific neighborhood and is just what they were looking for. But soon after they move into the house, the couple's four-year-old son begins spending a lot of time playing with an imaginary friend he calls "the old man." At first, the parents aren't worried, because they figure it is common for children to have imaginary friends. But then strange things begin to happen. The little boy refuses to come to dinner because he would rather stay in the basement and play with his friend. He becomes rebellious and more withdrawn from the family. A rocking chair in the living room creaks back and forth, even though no one is in it. The smell of pipe tobacco often fills the air, although no one in the family smokes. The family cat growls and hisses, the fur stands up on the back of its neck, and it runs, terrified, from the room for no apparent reason.

One day, as the father is raking leaves in the yard, he strikes up a conversation with a neighbor. He tells the neighbor all about "the old man" and the strange goings-on in their house. The neighbor is curious. Could the little boy give a description of this imaginary friend? By the time the little boy finishes explaining what his new "friend" looks like, the color has drained from the neighbor's face, and his hands are shaking. The little boy has given a nearly perfect description of the former owner of the house. He was an elderly and unhappy man who, unbeknownst to the little boy or his parents, had committed suicide in the basement of their new home.

Had the unhappy old man come back to haunt the place of his death, or was something else at work in that old house in Pennsylvania?

ARE THEY FOR REAL?

There always seems to be at least one house in a neighborhood rumored to be haunted. Kids are fascinated with the idea, while adults usually brush it off as nothing more than over-zealous imaginations at work. What do you think about haunted houses, ghosts, and such?

I know from experience that they are quite real. There are ghostly beings walking our planet today, seemingly appearing and disappearing at will, rattling chains in the deep darkness of the night, and sometimes moaning, groaning, and scaring people half to death. At other times, they try to win people over by showing their "wisdom" and "love." But these are not ghosts or spirits of people who have died. Even though a "haunted house" may be a scary, fascinating place, the real purpose of these "creatures of the night" is even more frightening—something much worse than disembodied spirits.

In situations like those described above, you are dealing with demons—beings who are bound and determined to further the kingdom of their lord and master, Satan. When we talk about demons, most people will laugh at us. Even people who are willing to believe in ghosts may make fun of us if we say we believe in demons. Intellectuals say demons don't exist—that the very term is a relic from a bygone age, when physical and mental illnesses were thought to be the work of supernatural forces. "These days," they'll tell you, "we know better, and what used to be thought of as demons are really nothing more than the strange workings of the human mind and body."

But those intellectuals are wrong—very wrong. Demons do exist, and they are doing everything within their power to destroy as many souls as they possibly can. Demonic forces are on a rampage, because they know they are about to be destroyed forever. We are definitely living in the end times. As the thousand-year reign of Jesus draws closer, their annihilation is also drawing closer, and they are determined to take as many people into eternal destruction with them as they can.

DEMONS AT WORK

Demons take pride in a job well done when teenage gangs take control of our city streets and when kids eleven and twelve years of age commit murder and other violent crimes. The entertainment industry has sold out to sex, violence, and the degradation of the human spirit—all because the world wants to see it. America murders millions upon millions of innocent unborn children every year, with the attitude, *How dare we tell a woman what she can and cannot do to her body.*

Demons operate on a global scale, controlling politics, mass movements, and governments. But they also operate on a personal scale. If a demon can find a way to gain entrance into a person's life, he is going to do his very best to gain total control over that person. Demons oppress and harass their victims in a variety of ways. They may impersonate dead loved ones. They may "haunt" houses or other places. They may rattle chains in the middle of the night and make groaning noises. Or they may attempt to gain control over their victims' minds by pretending to be wise and benevolent spirits from a "higher plane." They may also possess a person.

WHAT SHOULD MY RESPONSE BE?

Greater is he that is in you, than he that is in the world.

(1 John 4:4)

[God] *disarmed the principalities and powers that were ranged against us and made a bold display and public example of them, in triumphing over them in Him and in it* [the cross].

(Colossians 2:15 AMP)

It is important to understand that if you are a born-again, Spirit-filled Christian, you don't have a single thing to fear from demonic forces. It doesn't matter if every demon in the universe, including Satan himself, is against us; all of the forces of hell must bow at the name of Jesus.

Our focus must be on the Lord, not on Satan. However, we gain nothing by ignoring demonic forces. Ignorance can be extremely dangerous. Demons are very active in the world today, and when we choose to ignore demons, we give them free reign to do whatever they want to do. We need to be aware that demons exist and what their tactics are if we want to overcome them. The satanic world has a government, a purpose, and a vision for what it seeks to accomplish. Satan, also known as Lucifer, is as busy today as he has ever been. His one desire is to destroy all human beings, including you and me. So as born-again, Spirit-filled Christians, sooner or later we are going to come face-to-face with demonic forces in one way or another. When that happens, we need to know what to do.

Then he called his twelve disciples together, and gave them power and authority over all devils, and to cure diseases.

(Luke 9:1)

The good news is that we have been given authority through Jesus to overcome the forces of hell, to protect ourselves and our loved ones from satanic onslaught, and to help others gain deliverance from the forces of evil.

BE AWARE

Perhaps you're a sweet girl whom everyone thinks of as being very feminine and not the least bit warrior-like. You can still have victory over all the forces of hell through the power of Jesus Christ. Perhaps you're a businessman who wears a three-piece suit to work every day and sits behind a desk. You too can recognize demonic activity in the lives of your co-workers or your clients and deal with it, helping to set them free forever.

Few things in this world are sadder or more pathetic than someone who is held hostage by a demon. Such people may go through life confused, not understanding why they do so many things they don't really want to do, never realizing the demon or demons inside them cause them to act in such ways. Or they may be well aware they are demonized. They may hear voices and be subject to other strange phenomena, but they simply don't know what to do about it. They don't know the power of God can set them free.

> *The Spirit of the Lord is upon me, because he hath anointed me to preach the gospel to the poor; he hath sent me to heal the brokenhearted, to preach deliverance to the captives, and recovering of sight to the blind, to set at liberty them that are bruised.* (Luke 4:18)

Because we are commanded to follow in Jesus' footsteps, we also need to be about the business of preaching deliverance—setting free those who are held hostage by Satan and his armies from hell. We are not to go around looking for demons, but we can learn to deal with demons swiftly, powerfully, and correctly by using the authority we have in Jesus Christ.

Demons in the Church

One encounter I will never forget happened at a one-night meeting in St. Louis. When I got up to preach, demons were the farthest thing from my mind. My intention was to talk about the glories of heaven. Then, halfway through my planned sermon, the Spirit of God spoke to me and said, "I want to cast out devils tonight."

What? I had been invited to talk about heaven. I wasn't sure how my hosts would react if I suddenly took a 180-degree turn and started dealing with the forces of hell instead. But when God spoke, I listened and obeyed. If God wanted me to cast out devils, then I was going to cast out devils. It became apparent very quickly why God was directing me this way—it was because there were so many of them in the auditorium! Hundreds of people were there, and most of them seemed to be accompanied by their own personal demons.

All of a sudden, it was like a wind swept through the room, and people all over began to react violently. Some yelled and screamed, some sobbed, others fell to the ground and rolled around, and a few slithered across the floor like snakes. My attention was soon focused on a big, burly man standing in the back of the room. He was glaring straight at me with nothing but hatred in his eyes. He didn't say it, but I knew he was thinking, *I'm going to kill you!* Before I knew it, he was running down the aisle full-speed ahead, coming straight toward me. Now there were a number of ushers in the auditorium, but no one was about to get in the way of this huge, demon-possessed man, running as fast as he could, intent on trampling anyone who tried to stop him. I just stood there, watching him charge, and braced for the collision.

Meanwhile, on the stage behind me was another preacher who had been part of the program that night. Although he was not in the best physical shape, he ran past me, jumped off the six-foot high stage without stumbling, and headed straight for the man who was streaking toward me. I didn't care how big the demon-possessed man was or how many demons he had in him—I knew he wasn't going to be any match for one overweight preacher operating with the Spirit of God.

That preacher made such a great diving tackle, you would have thought he was a lineman for the as Cowboys. *Bam!* The man hit the floor, cursing and growling and thrashing about. In a matter of minutes, several the ushers come out of their hiding places to help. They grabbed the man and held him up against the wall so they could minister to him.

The entire time they were casting the demon out of him, you could hear him screaming and yelling, threatening to kill everyone in the room. By the time he was finally set free, there was a huge dent where he had been banging his head against the wall—a steel wall! That is the sort of thing a demon can do to a human being.

DEMONS ON A ROOFTOP

On another occasion, when I was living in Tulsa, Oklahoma, I got a call from a woman who was on the edge of hysteria. Her fourteen-year-old son had become violent, had beaten her, and had thrown her into a corner. When his father tried to discipline him, the boy knocked the father to the ground and began beating him. This was no wimpy father. He was over six feet tall and looked strong enough to hold his own in any fair fight. But he was no match for his young son, who was not nearly as tall or as strong as his father, but who had a supernatural strength due to demonic possession.

When I got to their house, the parents told me their son's abusive behavior had been going on for some time. I could see they were telling me the truth by the number of holes in the wall, the smashed lamps, and the numerous pieces of broken furniture. This attack had apparently been more severe, and the mother was in the kitchen, crying and shaking from fear. As I walked into the kitchen, I felt the authority of God come on me. It came over the top of me and went down to the bottom of my feet. I felt like even my toes had power, and I not a power on earth could stand against me.

"Where is he?" I asked her.

"He's on the roof."

That's exactly where I found him—on the roof with a can of gasoline and a book of matches, pouring the gasoline all around and threatening to set the house on fire.

"What are you doing up there?" I asked him.

"I'm trying to burn the house," he replied.

"Really?" I looked at him for a moment, and then said, "You're not going to do any such thing. You come down from there."

He just glared at me. "I'm not coming down."

"If you don't get down right now, I'm going to come up there and knock you off."

"You wouldn't dare." He spit the words at me in a hate-filled challenge.

All this happened on a Sunday morning, and I was wearing one of my favorite suits. At the moment, though, that didn't matter. I knew I had to go up on the roof to get that kid.

By the time I got up there, he had climbed down as fast as he could, had run into his bedroom, and had slammed the door behind him. I followed him as fast as I could. When I got to his bedroom, he was lying in a fetal position in the corner, whining and moaning in a strange little voice.

He wouldn't turn around and look at me, so I reached over, grabbed him, and "unwrapped" him into the middle of the floor. As I began praying for him, laying hands on him, and using the name of Jesus, he went into a position that I can only describe as looking like he was being nailed to a cross. And he began to moan and scream, acting as if I was killing him. I continued to pray for him, and he began to growl deep, guttural sounds, like a dog about to attack. But I didn't let go of him, and I didn't quit praying for him.

This went on for about an hour. I couldn't get him to look at me, and when I turned his head toward me to get his attention, he closed his eyes as tight as possible. But I wasn't about to quit on him. I continued to pray over him and cast the demons out of him. It was quite a battle, but through the power of Jesus, he was eventually set free.

Once I had cast out the demon, I still had the flesh to deal with. One of the ways demons gain access to people's lives is when people develop an unnatural craving for something they are lacking. The evil spirit will oblige that craving by giving a false satisfaction. In this instance, I discerned that the boy was craving attention and affection from his parents. After the evil spirit was cast out of him, I still had to deal with the boy's fleshly pattern of behavior. I also prayed for the boy's mother and father, that they would be able to deal properly with their son and feel free to show their love for him.

A few weeks later, the young man came to church where I was preaching, sat in the second row with his Bible on his lap, and took notes. The difference between the first and second time I saw him was literally the difference between night and day. It is amazing what the power of Satan can do to a human being, but it is even more amazing to see the difference the power of God can make in a person's life.

The late preacher, Lester Sumrall, told the story of what happened when he was conducting a crusade in the Philippines. He was listening to the radio when an urgent appeal was made to anyone who could help a young girl who was in very desperate need. The announcer wasn't clear as to what was wrong with the girl, but the fear and urgency in his voice implied that it was something terrible. In the background, Brother Sumrall could hear the young girl screaming and carrying on the way you might expect from someone who was under a demonic attack.

As he listened to the terrible wailing, Brother Sumrall heard the Lord's voice saying, "Go and cast the devil out of her."

He told the Lord this wasn't something he wanted to do, "Please, Lord, let someone else cast the demon out of her."

The reply was not judgmental, but it was firm "You are the only one here who knows how to deal with this situation. Go!"

When God speaks to you like that, you have no choice but to obey, so Brother Sumrall went down to meet the girl and do as the Lord had commanded. It seemed this young girl was serving time in a Philippine prison. Her background included prostitution and drug addiction, and she had opened herself up to all sorts of evil influences.

When Brother Sumrall got to the prison, he found a young woman writhing and squirming in agony, panting and gasping for breath. Even more astonishing, teeth marks suddenly began appearing on the surface of her skin. Some unseen demon was actually attacking and biting the girl. She would push at the air, as if she was fighting to get something off of her, screaming, "They're biting me again!"

Surrounding the girl were reporters, doctors, witch doctors, and priests, all of whom wanted to help her, but all of whom seemed to be completely helpless in the face of her agony. One of the reporters told Brother Sumrall that a couple of days earlier the girl had cursed two of her "enemies," and they had died inexplicably the very next day. No wonder all of those who were standing around watching this pathetic scene were terrified!

It wasn't easy to get this girl free. Brother Sumrall cast the demons out of her, but because of the life she was living and her reluctance to give her heart to Jesus, even after she was set free, the demons kept coming back into her. For the next three days, Brother Sumrall went down to where she was, prayed for her, had her confess her sins, and cast the demons out of her. On the day the spirits came out of her for good, he had everyone on their knees singing, "Oh, the Blood of Jesus." Thankfully, she was set free once and for all and was able to get out of prison and live a happy, moral Christian life thereafter.

You can do the same thing Lester Sumrall did. If you belong to Jesus, you have the same power within you that he had during those days in the Philippians. No matter what the demons may do, no matter how they may manifest themselves, you can defeat them through the power and blood of Jesus.

MULTIPLIED DEMONS

Before we move on to a discussion of what demons are and where they come from, let me give you an example from the October 25, 1982, issue of *Time* magazine. The article is titled, "The Twenty-Seven Faces of Charles." It tells the story of a young man, twenty-nine years of age, who was found wandering in a dazed condition on the beach near Daytona Beach, Florida. The paramedics who found him thought he was mentally handicapped, so they took him to the local hospital. At the hospital, the young man astonished the doctors by speaking to them in two distinct voices. The first voice was that of a scared little boy who claimed he was being abused. The second was that of an intelligent and articulate adult. The young man was kept at the hospital for observation, and soon other personalities began to manifest themselves through him. He would sometimes snarl, growl, scream, and curse violently.

Dr. Graham, the hospital psychiatrist, recorded more than two hundred conversations with the young man, during which a total of twenty-nine different entities spoke through him. There was a young man named Mark, another one named Dwight, a blind mute called Jeffrey, an arrogant jock who said he was Michael, a woman named Tina, another female who said she was a lesbian, and a religious mystic who often spoke in terms associated with New Age philosophy. These different entities did not get along and would often fight each other. One of them, named T. K., who was especially angry, would sometimes do bodily harm to their host.

You can see from this example that demons really are crazy. They are so full of hatred and anger that they can't get along with anyone or anything, including each other. They are united only in their hatred for God, their fear and contempt for the blood of Jesus, and their desire to destroy the human race.

Of course, the doctors who dealt with this young man who had twenty-nine different entities speaking through him would never tell you he was possessed by evil spirits, because they don't believe in demons. Instead, they talk in terms of split personalities and malfunctions of the brain. That is sad, because what was going on with this young man was clear and simple—he had given demons entrance into his life, and they were tearing him apart. He didn't need a bunch of doctors sitting around analyzing him or getting him to lie down on a couch and talk about his childhood.

He needed a born-again, Spirit-filled believer to introduce him to Jesus and show him how he could be set free forever. He needed a personal encounter with Jesus.

Earlier, I asked if you believe in ghosts, haunted houses, and such. Now I have another question: Do you believe demons exist? You should, because they are every bit as real as you and me. Whenever you hear or read of haunted houses and ghostly manifestations, you can know beyond any doubt that demons are involved. The world doesn't understand this, and for that reason, it is ripe for seduction and betrayal. The world talks of split personalities, parapsychology, or earth-bound spirits. But a war is raging on this planet between darkness (demonic forces) and light (Christianity), and whether you realize it or not, you are either on one side or the other. You are either fighting for God, or you are fighting against God.

The good news is that if you are a born-again believer, you have the authority and power to stand against demonic forces through Jesus and His Word.

No weapon that is formed against thee shall prosper.

(Isaiah 54:17)

Finally, my brethren, be strong in the Lord, and in the power of his might. Put on the whole armor of God, that ye may be able to stand against the wiles of the devil.

(Ephesians 6:10–11)

CHAPTER 2

THE FALL FROM GLORY

We have established that demons exist and that they are bent on the destruction of humankind. But where do demons come from? Who created them? And who is their leader? To find the answer to these questions, we have to go back before the creation of humanity and before God spoke this planet of ours into existence. Sometime way back there, and we really don't know when, God created the glorious creatures called angels. Chief among these were the archangels, including Gabriel, Michael, and another powerful being by the name of Lucifer.

> *You were in Eden, the garden of God; every precious stone was your covering: The sardius, topaz, and diamond, beryl, onyx, and jasper, sapphire, turquoise, and emerald with gold. The workmanship of your timbrels and pipes was prepared for, you on the day you were created. You were the anointed cherub who covers; I established you; you were on the holy mountain of God; you walked back and forth in the midst of fiery stones. You were perfect in your, ways from the day you were created, till iniquity was found in you. By the abundance of your trading you became filled with violence within, and you sinned; therefore I cast you as a profane thing out of the mountain of God; and I destroyed you, O covering cherub,*

from the midst of the fiery stones. Your, heart was lifted up because of your, beauty, you corrupted your, wisdom for the sake of your splendor; I cast you to the ground, I laid you before kings, that they might gaze at you.

(Ezekiel 28:13–17 NKJV)

Some speculate that Lucifer was possibly the most powerful of all the archangels. Whether that is true or not, we know he was an intelligent, beautiful, and proud creature. He must have received a lot of recognition and praise from the other angels, and it went right to his head.

Lucifer was a near-perfect creature, but he began to think he was responsible for his own power and beauty. If we were to put it into the modern vernacular, we might say Lucifer began to believe his own press release. And it's a dangerous game when you start to believe and act upon the good things other people say about you. We stay balanced when we believe and act upon what God says about us and what He has called us to. Don't take the accolades of people too seriously. (See James 1:16–17.)

Lucifer became so puffed up with pride that he decided he could do a better job of ruling the universe than God Himself. Apparently, some of the other angels felt the same way. Lucifer probably began to tell them what he would do if he was in charge, how he would make life better for them, and in this way he planted seeds of rebellion throughout the ranks of the angels.

How these angels ever thought they could actually overthrow God is beyond my comprehension. Surely they knew there was really no way they could ever defeat Him. I don't understand how they ever could have rebelled against God after living so close to Him on a daily basis. They were firsthand witnesses to His amazing power and overwhelming love for all of creation. It shows what a destructive force pride can be.

*How you are fallen from heaven, O Lucifer, son of the morn-
ing! How you are cut down to the ground, you who weakened
the nations! For, you have said in your heart: "I will ascend
into heaven, I will exalt my throne above the stars of God; I
will also sit on the mount of the congregation on the farthest
sides of the north; I will ascend above the heights of the clouds,
I will be like the Most High." Yet you shall be brought down to
Sheol, to the lowest depths of the Pit.*

(Isaiah 14:12–15 NKJV)

From certain Scriptures, we can ascertain that as many as
one-third of the angels joined Lucifer in his rebellion. In a battle
that raged throughout the universe, they were defeated and banished from heaven forever. These fallen angels are what we know
as *demons* or *devils.* Many have the idea that demons are hideous
creatures with ugly contorted faces, bat-like wings, and horns
growing out of their heads. But that's hardly the truth. Lucifer was
a beautiful and powerful creature. (See Ezekiel 28:12–13.)

*And no marvel; for, Satan himself is transformed into an
angel of light.* (2 Corinthians 11:14)

Lucifer is able to transform himself into an angel of light. In
fact, his very name means "the Lightbearer."[1] If he was an ugly and
scary-looking being, no one would be attracted to him. But like
sin, he looks pretty good until you get close enough for him to
ensnare you.

Lucifer is so deluded by his own power that he still believes
he has a chance to wrest control of the universe away from God
Almighty. But when Lucifer and his followers were kicked out of
heaven, their fate was sealed for eternity. When Jesus rose from

---

1. James Strong, *The Exhaustive Concordance of the Bible* (Nashville: Abingdon, 1890), Hebrew and Chaldee Dictionary, #1966.

the dead, following His crucifixion, He pounded the final nail into Lucifer's coffin.

As we look around us, it would seem he could certainly take some fiendish pride in what he has been able to accomplish on this planet, but whatever he is able to do here is only because his time of eternal destruction has not yet come. But it is drawing very near. Until the final battle of Armageddon, Lucifer and his armies of darkness will continue in their rebellion, doing their best to deceive and destroy people.

When God created angels, He gave them free will to feel, think, and act for themselves. He did the same thing when He created humankind. He wants us to love and serve Him, not because we *have* to but because we *want* to. If the angels had been robots, Lucifer never would have rebelled. If human beings had been automatons, Adam and Eve never would have eaten the forbidden fruit in the Garden of Eden. But God has always believed in letting His creatures make their own choices, and in the case of Lucifer, his choice was to rebel.

Lucifer was not happy with who he was or with the way God had made him, and so he said, "I will become like the Most High." In today's world, a lot of people are not happy with the way God has made them. People are unhappy with everything from their socioeconomic status to the color of their hair. Some men don't want to be men, so they have operations to turn themselves into women (although they're really not women, just mutilated men). And some women want to be men. Some black people want to be white, and some white people want to be black. Such discontent always leads to trouble, and it always borders on the sort of rebellion that shakes a fist at God and says, "I could have done a better job." It's just not so.

Let's take one more look at what the Bible has to say about Lucifer's fall from grace.

*And his tail drew the third part of the star's of heaven, and did
cast them to the earth: and the dragon stood before the woman
which was ready to be delivered, for to devour her child as soon
as it was born…And there was war in heaven: Michael and
his angels fought against the dragon; and the dragon fought
and his angels. And prevailed not, neither, was their place
found any more in heaven. And the great dragon was cast out,
that old serpent, called the Devil, and Satan, which deceiveth
the whole world: he was cast out into the earth, and his angels
were cast out with him.* (Revelation 12:4, 7–9)

The dragon is Lucifer, who did his very best to destroy the
Christ child as soon as He was born. Remember how Herod
ordered the killing of all male children under two years of age?
(See Matthew 2:16.)

THE GREAT TRICKSTER

*Now the serpent was more subtle than any beast of the field
which the* LORD *God had made. And he said unto the woman,
Yea, hath God said, Ye shall not eat of every tree of the garden?
And the woman said unto the serpent, We may eat of the fruit
of the trees of the garden: but of the fruit of the tree which is in
the midst of the garden, God hath said, Ye shall not eat of it,
neither, shall ye touch it, lest ye die. And the serpent said unto
the woman, Ye shall not surely die: for God doth know that in
the day ye eat thereof, then your eyes shall be opened, and ye
shall be as gods, knowing good and evil.* (Genesis 3:1–5)

In this first encounter between Lucifer and humankind,
Lucifer used a talking snake to entice humankind into sin, thereby
bringing sickness, disease, and all sorts of terrible things into the
perfect world God had created. Adam and Eve fell from grace

by disobeying God. That was thousands of years ago, but today Lucifer is still using the same tricks of deception to get people to turn away from God. And if he can't do it subtly, by telling us lies and tempting us with tasty looking sins, he'll do it by attempting to grab hold of us and taking control of our bodies and souls.

The greatest desire of any demon is to gain entrance into the soul, the spirit, and the body of a human being and take up residence. We have been created in God's image (see Genesis 1:26–27), and gaining control of someone who has been created in God's image is a source of tremendous joy to one of these citizens of hell.

NAMES OF SATAN

I emphasize again that it is not good to think too much about Lucifer or his demon armies. We don't want to give him too much credit; neither do we want to focus on him when we really need to keep our attention fastened on God and His Word. But at the same time, we need to know as much as we can about Lucifer in order to fend off his attacks and outsmart him. One of the best ways we can learn about him is by taking a look at some of the names the Bible gives him. The following are only a few of Lucifer's names, but they will give us a better understanding of his personality and his plan.

THE PRINCE OF THE AIR

Wherein in time past ye walked according to the course of this world, according to the prince of the power, of the air, the spirit that now worketh in the children of disobedience.

(Ephesians 2:2)

According to Paul's writings, there are three heavens. (See Ephesians 4:10.) The first is the earth's atmosphere, the second is the spirit world (or the heavens where there are spirit beings), and the third heaven is the planet called heaven, where all Christians are going to go eventually. The home of Lucifer is the second heaven, in the spirit world where he rules with his principalities.

THE PRINCE OF DARKNESS

For we wrestle not against flesh and blood, but against principalities, against powers, against the rulers of the darkness of this world, against spiritual wickedness in high places.

(Ephesians 6:12)

It's understandable that Lucifer would love the darkness, because it helps to cover up his evil deeds. He's not the type of creature to be out there in the bright sunshine, because it would reveal him for who and what he is. He stays in the shadows, slinking around under the cover of the night. Unconfessed sin is a type of darkness, and it will attract evil spirits. Hurts and wounds that remain unforgiven and have not been healed properly are a form of darkness, and they too will attract Lucifer and his armies.

But if we walk in the light, as he is in the light, we have fellowship one with another, and the blood of Jesus Christ his Son cleanseth us from all sin. (1 John 1:7)

If you are going to be strong, you must live in the light—the light of God's Word and obedience to Him. Lucifer and his followers cannot stand the light, and they will flee from you.

THE PRINCE OF THIS WORLD

Now is the judgment of this world: now shall the prince of this world be cast out. (John 12:31)

Lucifer earned this title when he tempted Adam and Eve to turn away from God, and it is a title he will hold until the end times, when he will be thrown into the lake of fire and utterly banished once and for all. When Jesus Christ returns to rule and reign, He will take His rightful place as the King and Prince of this world, but until that glorious day, Lucifer still has claim to much of this planet.

THE PRINCE OF DEVILS

But when the Pharisees heard it, they said, This fellow doth
not cast out devils, but by Beelzebub the prince of the devils.
(Matthew 12:24)

I think it would be terrible to be prince over a bunch of devils. You can bet Lucifer always has to look behind him, because he doesn't have any friends. It's probably true that every devil in the universe thinks he could do a better job in the war against God. Lucifer is a rebel and a liar who is surrounded by rebels and liars.

THE GOD OF THIS WORLD

In whom the god of this world hath blinded the minds of them
which believe not, lest the light of the glorious gospel of Christ,
who is the image of God, should shine unto them.
(2 Corinthians 4:4)

This is very much like the prince of this world, but it connotes even more of an authority over this planet. Lucifer is not really a god; he just wants to be one. But until the kingdom of heaven is ushered in with the dawning of the millennium, Lucifer and his forces exercise a great deal of control here.

AN ANGEL OF LIGHT

*And no marvel; for Satan himself is transformed into an angel
of light.*   (2 Corinthians 11:14)

Sometimes Lucifer's lies contain just enough truth to make
the whole thing look real. He's the master at making what's wrong
look right and vice versa. If he revealed himself to us the way he
really is, we would find very little about him appealing, so he comes
to us in sweetness and light, saying, as he did to Adam and Eve,
"I know what God said, but He doesn't really mean it. What He
really means is...." And he leads us down the road of deception and
destruction. But if you know God and are standing solidly upon
His Word, you will not be taken in by the false light Lucifer tries
to bring your way.

Joseph Smith, the founder of the Mormon religion, claimed
to have been visited by angels of light. They told him where he
could find the tablets that were later translated into the Book of
Mormon. If Joseph Smith had known about Lucifer's ability to
transform himself into an angel of light, he probably never would
have written the Book of Mormon, and millions of innocent
people would not have been led down the path of destruction by
a false religion! So beware! Although he is the prince of darkness, Lucifer can and often does transform himself into an angel
of light.

THE SERPENT

*But I fear, lest by any means, as the serpent beguiled Eve
through his subtlety, so your minds should be corrupted from
the simplicity that is in Christ.*   (2 Corinthians 11:3)

There is nothing sneakier or slipperier than a snake! Satan tempted Eve by reasoning with her, corrupting her mind, and convincing her God was holding back true knowledge from her and Adam. If you are making decisions that are contrary to the Word of God, stop! Do not listen to those who try to sway you from your devotion and commitment to the Lord.

OUR ADVERSARY

Be sober, be vigilant; because your adversary the devil, as a roaring lion, walketh about, seeking whom he may devour.
(1 Peter 5:8)

We have no common ground with Lucifer. He has been our enemy from the beginning and always will be. Years ago, the rock group, The Rolling Stones, recorded a song called, "Sympathy for the Devil." Don't go feeling sorry for Lucifer, because he doesn't feel sorry for you, and he wouldn't think twice about destroying you. He is your adversary, and he *hates* you.

THE ACCUSER OF THE BRETHREN

And I heard a loud voice saying in heaven, Now is come salvation, and strength, and the kingdom of out God, and the power of his Christ: for the accuser of our brethren is cast down, which accused them before our God day and night.
(Revelation 12:10)

Satan loves to point a finger at you and tell your heavenly Father what a terrible person you are. He's quick to expose all the sins you've committed. Think of him as an evil prosecuting attorney who is pointing out all your crimes and demanding that God punish you for them. But if you have been washed in the blood of Jesus, all God sees in you is the righteousness of His Son, Jesus Christ.

As Lucifer is ranting, raving, and accusing you of all sorts of crimes worthy of punishment by death, God looks at you and says, "I don't know what in the world you're talking about, Lucifer. This person looks totally innocent to me."

> *For he hath made him to be sin for us, who knew no sin; that we might be made the righteousness of God in him.*
>
> (2 Corinthians 5:21)

> *And be found in him, not having mine own righteousness, which is of the law, but that which is through the faith of Christ, the righteousness which is of God by faith.*
>
> (Philippians 3:9)

Praise God for the righteousness that is ours through faith in Christ! Go ahead and accuse, Lucifer.

Another way Lucifer accuses is by spreading false rumors He loves to get people whispering about one another behind their backs, spreading and believing lies about one another. Friends, you must be very careful what you listen to and strive to give your brothers and sisters in Christ the benefit of the doubt. When you hear something terrible about someone, just remember that Lucifer is the accuser of the brethren.

> *Therefore, as God's chosen people, holy and dearly loved, clothe yourselves with compassion, kindness, humility, gentleness and patience. Bear with each other and forgive one another if any of you has a grievance against someone. Forgive as the Lord forgave you.* (Colossians 3:12–13 NIV)

THE TEMPTER

And when the tempter came to him, he said, If thou be the Son
of God, command that these stones be made bread.

(Matthew 4:3)

Lucifer tempted Adam and Eve to sin in the Garden of Eden, and he's been tempting as many people as possible ever since then. Being tempted does not make you guilty of sin. We are all tempted. You're only guilty of sin when you give in to temptation. Hebrews 4:15 tells us Jesus was tempted by every temptation known to humanity, but He did not act on them and sin.

You may be able to resist temptation the first time it comes, but Lucifer doesn't give up. He'll keep coming back and tempting you over and over again if you let him. Sometimes the temptation grows stronger and becomes harder to resist as time goes by. Adultery, for example, is like that. It may start out by simply thinking that some woman (or man) is nice or sweet or good-looking. You're tempted to flirt a little, but you think of it as innocent fun; it won't really hurt anyone. How about if you ask her out for coffee or an innocent lunch? With each step, you're flirting with danger. The temptation becomes more and more difficult to resist, until you find yourself in a full-blown affair, wondering how in the world you got there.

You got there by giving in to your flesh again and again instead of recognizing the temptation and submitting yourself immediately to God. When you do this, you can then receive His wisdom and strength to resist the devil.

Submit yourselves therefore to God. Resist the devil, and he
will flee from you.   (James 4:7)

THE THIEF

The thief cometh not, but for, to steal, and to kill, and to destroy: I am come that they might have life, and that they might have it more abundantly.　　　　(John 10:10)

Lucifer is a thief. He will steal your money, your health, your joy, your family relationships, your position in the kingdom of God, and your vision and passion for God's work. He would steal your very salvation if he could. Lucifer loves to steal, and he loves to get other people to steal too. Kleptomaniacs are people who can't help but steal things. It doesn't really matter what it is. It may be something they don't have the slightest use for, but they see it and just have to have it. The world calls this a sickness, but such people are really controlled by an evil spirit that likes to steal.

THE MURDERER

Ye are of your, father the devil, and the lusts of your, father ye will do. He was a murderer from the beginning, and abode not in the truth, because there is no truth in him. When he speaketh a lie, he speaketh of his own: for he is a liar, and the father of it.　　　　(John 8:44)

Satan has killed every human being who has ever died on this planet. What do I mean? If it wasn't for the fall of man in the Garden of Eden, there wouldn't be any such thing as death. We would all live forever, joyously in the presence of God.

Satan is also a murderer in a more specific sense. He wants people to hate each other and kill each other. He delights in the teen gangs that engage in drive-by shootings, who think nothing of killing others just because they're not wearing the right color of clothes. Satan also takes great joy in the millions of abortions that are performed in this world each year. By murdering children, he is destroying the next generation of leaders and revivalists. He killed the children when Moses was born and again when Jesus was born. It's so sad to think that some of our greatest preachers may have been murdered before they were ever able to take their first breath! Ultimately, murder takes place in the destruction of the souls of people. Satan wants to take as many as possible with him into his place of torment. He wants to destroy your soul.

There are also specific murdering demons who seek to kill and injure. I have read news stories about a murder in which the killer was quoted as saying, "I just wanted to kill someone," or, "I just wanted to see what it felt like to kill someone." When people say something like that, you can be fairly positive they have come under the influence of murdering demons.

I have heard demons say, "I'm a demon who loves the taste and the smell of blood. I love to spill blood." This is a murdering spirit. I have especially had to deal with them when I've been in foreign regions of the world, such as in Africa and Europe. In countries where there have been many civil wars and rebellions, some of the soldiers get so used to the spilling of human blood that they open themselves up to demonic influence. Some of these soldiers actually become addicted to killing.

The country of Uganda went through horror under a man named Idi Amin. Shortly after he was driven from power, I was in that country and went down into the dungeon underneath the capitol building in Kampala. There were still blood stains on the walls. Amin and his soldiers would torture and kill those they considered to be their enemies and then practice cannibalism. They would actually butcher those people like they were cattle, take their flesh home, and eat it. How can we explain such horrible behavior?

We can only explain it as the murdering nature of Lucifer and his demon armies.

Demons are vicious, horrendous fiends. Yet we have nothing to fear so long as we are walking in the power of the Lord.

A ROARING LION

Be alert and of sober mind. Your enemy the devil prowls around like a roaring lion looking for someone to devour.

(1 Peter 5:8 NIV)

Most of us see lions in only two places—the zoo and the circus. As long as they're kept behind iron bars in their cages, they're not that scary. But I certainly wouldn't want to meet one out in the wild. Lions are huge cats. Have you ever watched a cat stalk its prey? It crouches down and waits silently, almost without breathing, twitching its tail ever so slightly and looking for the right moment to strike. Suddenly, it leaps into action and is on top of its prey before the poor victim has a chance to even think about escaping. That's a very good description of Lucifer. He waits, he watches, and he looks for the exact moment to strike. It may be that one moment of weakness, that split second of carelessness. He's crouched, he's waiting, and he's looking to devour you. Be alert!

TALENTS OF DEMONS

Individual demons have differing personalities, but they all have a particular area of wickedness—a certain specialty with which they seek to inflict human beings. As I wrote about the existence of murdering spirits, there are other specific types of demons.

Familiar Spirits

*Regard not them that have familiar, spirits, neither, seek after
wizards, to be defiled by them: I am the LORD your God.*
(Leviticus 19:31)

The Bible warns us to avoid familiar spirits. A familiar spirit is
a demon involved in activities such as séances and fortune-telling.
It is called a familiar spirit because it is familiar with everything
about you and your ancestors! Very often it will imitate the personalities of dead human beings. A spirit medium almost always
has a spirit guide. When the medium goes into a trance, the spirit
guide takes over and controls the rest of the séance. Usually this
spirit guide will pretend to be an ancient, wise, and benevolent
being. It may be ancient, but it is not wise or benevolent! It is a
demon—what the Bible calls a familiar spirit.

A Blind Spirit

This is a demon that can cause physical and spiritual blind-
ness. (See Matthew 12:22.) I have seen the eyes of blind people
opened by the casting out of this spirit. It is truly an amazing
thing when someone suddenly has vision, perhaps for the first
time in that person's life. When all the colors, lights, and visual
sensations sink into that person's brain, it is like seeing someone
being born.

A Lying Spirit

This is simply a demon that makes people lie. (See 1 Kings
22:21–23.) You can give this particular demon entrance into your
life just by telling a few lies. Parents must teach their children at
an early age to tell the truth. If we don't teach them the importance
of honesty and truthfulness, they will become liars, and a lying
spirit will get hold of them. When children lie to avoid getting
into trouble for something they've done, and they get away with it,

they'll see how the lie benefited them. They will soon believe a lie can be better than the truth, and that opens the door for a lying spirit to walk through.

Sometimes a lying spirit or other demon will get into young children's lives but stay pretty much hidden until they grow up. Then it will manifest itself and cause all kinds of problems for these individuals, their friends, and their family. Parents, for your children's sake, please watch carefully over them in this area.

A Seducing Spirit

Now the Spirit speaketh expressly, that in the latter, times some shall depart from the faith, giving heed to seducing spirits, and doctrines of devils. (1 Timothy 4:1)

A seducing spirit is a demon that will tempt you to reject God's truth. This spirit may try to seduce you into immoral sexual activity. But it is just as likely to try to seduce you into intellectualism and rejection of God's truth, because you've become "too smart to believe all that." You must always be on your guard against such spirits.

A Binding Spirit

Verily I say unto you, Whatsoever ye shall bind on earth shall be bound in heaven: and whatsoever ye shall loose on earth shall be loosed in heaven. (Matthew 18:18)

Have you ever felt like you were bound—like something had a hold of you and just wouldn't let go? Maybe you want to have more faith in God, but something is holding you back. You want to be happy, but you're just so sad. You may very well be in the grip of a binding spirit, but the power of God can set you free.

A Foul Spirit

This spirit is mentioned in Mark 9:25 and Revelation 18:22. It is not a misnomer. Some demons actually smell. They have a terrible stench, and sometimes you can smell them when you're casting them out. On occasion, I have actually gotten sick to my stomach when dealing with a foul spirit. It's not so much through the nose that you can smell them; instead, it's as if their stench almost overpowers your spirit.

A Jealous Spirit

Numbers 5:14 explains the spirit of jealousy. You've probably heard jealously described as a "green-eyed monster." That's not far from the truth. Jealousy is a beast that can kill relationships, churches, organizations, and people's lives. I have seen men of God virtually destroyed because someone became jealous of them or jealousy rose up within them. Jealousy is totally opposed to the Spirit of God, and if you give in to this type of demon, it can suck the life and joy right out of you.

A Religious Spirit

> For men shall be lovers of their own selves, covetous, boasters, proud, blasphemers, disobedient to parents, unthankful, unholy, without natural affection, trucebreakers, false accusers, incontinent, fierce, despiser's of those that are good, traitors, heady, high-minded, lover's of pleasures more than lovers of God; having a form of godliness, but denying the power thereof: from such turn away.   (2 Timothy 3:2–5)

Some think demons are afraid of a Christian church and won't go near it simply because it has a cross on the roof and Bibles in the pews. Let me assure you that this is very far from the truth! It is possible for demons to feel right at home in many of America's churches.

Some churches have forgotten why we get together on Sunday morning. They're into this cause and that cause, even supplying guns and ammunition to terrorist groups around the world. They have forgotten the simple truth that Jesus Christ died, was buried, and rose again on the third day, and through His sacrifice we can obtain forgiveness of our sins. They have what 2 Timothy 3:5 calls a form of godliness, but they don't know a thing about God's power.

Jesus told us we are supposed to be the salt of the earth. (See Matthew 5:13.) Then He said that if salt loses its saltiness, it is good for nothing, so you might as well throw it out and walk on it. That's exactly what has happened in many of our churches. They've completely lost their saltiness and have become easy prey for a religious spirit. When Jesus comes, He will tell these so-called Christians that they have never really known Him and that they are worthless, and He will cast them out. (See Matthew 7:22–23.)

I have discussed only a few of the many types of demons at work in this world. But it's not really necessary to know what sort of demon you're dealing with in order to cast it out. All demons are subject to the power and authority of Jesus. All must submit to the authority God gives to you as a born-again, Spirit-filled Christian. The plain fact is that if you belong to Jesus, Lucifer and all his demons are afraid of you. They hate you. They'd like to destroy you. But they know beyond any doubt that you're more powerful than they are.

Greater is he that is in you, than he that is in the world.

(1 John 4:4)

Go forward in the power and might of Jesus and conquer!

CHAPTER 3

A HABITATION OF DEMONS

And when he was come out of the ship, immediately there met him out of the tombs a man with an unclean spirit. Who had his dwelling among the tombs, and no man could bind him, no, not with chains: because that he had been often bound with fetters and chains, and the chains had been plucked asunder by him, and the fetters broken in pieces: neither could any man tame him. And always, night and day, he was in the mountains, and in the tombs, crying and cutting himself with stones. But when he saw Jesus afar off, he ran and worshipped him. And cried with a loud voice, and said, What have I to do with thee, Jesus, thou Son of the most high God? I adjure thee by God, that thou torment me not. For he said unto him, Come out of the man, thou unclean spirit. And he asked him, What is thy name? And he answered, saying, My name is Legion: for we are many. And he besought him much that he would not send them away out of the country. Now there was there nigh unto the mountains a great herd of swine feeding. And all the devils besought him, saying, Send us into the swine, that we may enter into them. And forthwith Jesus gave them leave. And the unclean spirits went out, and entered into the swine: and the herd ran violently down a steep place into

the sea, (they were about two thousand;) and were choked in
the sea.   (Mark 5:2–13)

Jesus and His disciples had come across the sea of Galilee into
the country of the Gadarenes. As soon as they arrived, they
were met by a demon-possessed man. This fellow lived among the
tombs—probably because the demons that had taken control of
him were more comfortable around death and decay than any-
where else. The people who lived nearby wanted desperately to
get rid of this man. Several times they attempted to capture him,
wrapping him with ropes and chains, but the demons made him so
strong that he was able to break the chains and escape.

It's interesting that as soon as Jesus got off the boat, this man
ran to Him, fell on his knees, and worshipped Him. The demons
within him recognized Jesus immediately, knew that He was the
Lord, and they weren't going to try to defy Him even for a moment.
They begged Jesus not to torment them before their time for judgment had come. The demons possessing this man knew Jesus was
going to cast them out, because they knew Jesus was sent to set the
captives free. (See Luke 4:18.) So they began looking frantically
for an alternative place where they could live. Looking around,
they spied a huge herd of pigs.

The Amplified version of verse 13 says Jesus gave them *per-
mission* to enter into the swine. Jesus has complete authority over
demon power. But something very unusual happened when they
went into those pigs. Those animals were so terrorized that they
ran down the hill and out into the sea, where they all drowned.

Imagine how terrified the pig farmer must have been! All of a
sudden, his pigs are going absolutely crazy. He's running around
trying to get them under control, but they're snorting, oinking,
and carrying on like a bunch of demon-possessed pigs—which is
exactly what they were! It must have been an amazing sight to see.

Can you imagine the story that pig farmer told the next time he was in town?

"Joseph, you're not going to believe this, but I was out with the pigs on an ordinary day when all of a sudden they just went crazy. They were whirling around and snorting and bucking like broncos. And then they all ran right into the sea and drowned!"

"All of them?"

"Every one of them!"

"Is this an April Fools' joke?"

"No, I'm telling you—it really happened!"

Most likely the pigs were frightened, they panicked, and wound up destroying themselves as a reaction to the demons entering their bodies. This shows us the end result of demonic possession—destruction. These "dumb" animals panicked at the sudden appearance of demons among them, but many human beings will open themselves to demonic influences and never give it a second thought. We even have people who worship Satan and invite demons to enter their spirits, souls, and bodies. Such total foolishness! You might as well put a sign in front of your house saying, "Thieves welcome! Come on in and steal us blind! Rob us! Kill us! Please!" It just doesn't make sense.

WHERE DO DEMONS LIVE?

Demons primarily reside in human beings, but if humans aren't available to them, they will go into animals. A demon wants to have a fleshly body, partly because he enjoys the sins of the flesh so much. A demon wants to fulfill the lusts of the flesh and the lust of the eyes. He wants to overeat, drink to excess, take drugs, and engage in all sorts of sexual perversions, and he needs a body to do these things. A human body is preferable, but if he has trouble getting one, he'll take whatever else is available to him.

If those two are unavailable, a demon will occupy a certain territory—an old house, a stretch of woods, an isolated lake. Our ancestors knew instinctively about these things. I'm sure your grandparents or older relatives told you stories when you were a small child of certain places they wouldn't go near, because they understood them to be evil places. Modern man has, to a great extent, stopped believing in such things. He has gotten too smart for his own good, too sophisticated for his own safety.

Years ago, I came across a true story about five college students who decided they were too smart and too sophisticated to believe in evil spirits, ghosts, or anything of the supernatural. They went out to a certain location near their school that was supposedly haunted and made fun of whatever spirits were present in that place. They ridiculed them, challenged them, and dared them to make their presence known. They thought this was all so much fun. Unfortunately, these students did not belong to Jesus. They thought those who believed in Jesus were just as foolish as those who believed in evil spirits. Because of their unbelief, they were not protected by the blood of Jesus, and the demons of that place apparently decided to take them up on their dare.

Within six months of their visit to the haunted area, all of the students had dropped out of school. Friends who knew them said they had become paranoid and fearful. They talked about strange things happening to them—hearing voices, seeing disembodied spirits, and feeling like their lives were in danger. Basically, those students went into hiding. Goals and dreams were abandoned. They had learned a very important lesson about the reality of the supernatural world, but they had learned it at a very great cost.

Now, I don't believe every so-called haunted house is actually the home of a demon or demons. Most haunted houses are nothing more than old buildings that have become a little run-down and creepy looking, and because they look a little scary, people let their imaginations run wild. But it is vitally important to understand that some haunted houses really are haunted. Almost always you'll find out that the demon was attracted to the place by some tragedy that happened there. Demons especially seem to be drawn by the spilling of human blood.

There are also places that have been dedicated to Satan. I know of an entire country that was dedicated to Satan—the tiny island nation of Haiti. Now Haiti is the poorest country in the Western Hemisphere, if not in the entire world, and it's a country that is very much into demonism. Haiti has been through a series of repressive governments. It's a place where you can still hear voodoo drums at night, and where, legend has it, zombies sometimes roam the countryside at night. I don't believe in zombies, but I do believe in the existence of demons and that they can manifest themselves in a variety of ways.

Some of Haiti's troubles can be traced back more than two hundred years to one of the governors of Haiti, who was a Satanist. He had an official ceremony in which he dedicated the country to the devil and effectively handed over Haiti to Satan's control. Haiti has had terrible trouble ever since. Of course, good Christian people still live in Haiti, but many more of Haiti's people are involved in voodooism and Satanism. There is an intense battle between the forces of good and evil in that country.

QUEST FOR POWER

There are also more specific areas where demons like to congregate. For example, demons love to be around the seat of political power. Demons love power. They've been hanging around kings, emperors, presidents, congressmen, and others with political power for as long as history has been recorded. That's not to say that there haven't been many fine men and women who have dedicated themselves to government service. But Christians who go into politics have a struggle in front of them, because they are surrounded by demonic influence.

If you read the history of the powerful kings and queens of old, you might be amazed by how many of them seemed to be absolutely crazy. Some were terribly cruel. Herod ordered all the little babies murdered. Nero murdered most of his own family and used human beings as torches to light his gardens. From biblical times right up until today, the world has seen many bloodthirsty tyrants. Wherever you find political power, you will also find demons.

I love this country, and I am proud to be an American. I thank God for the freedoms we enjoy here. I think Washington, D.C., is a beautiful and impressive city, but we're missing something important if we get dazzled by all the history, beauty, and power, and don't realize that the city of Washington has demonic activity. If you need more proof that political power and demons go together, think about the laws that come out of Washington— laws to restrict religious freedom, laws to make abortion easier and more readily available, laws to curtail the rights of parents, and laws to make it easier for criminals to get away with their crimes. Yes, indeed, Washington is influenced by the demonic powers of this world.

Years ago I read about a case in which the court took a young man away from his parents and placed him in a foster home because his parents were *forcing* him to go to Wednesday night Bible study at their church. The boy, who was fourteen at the time, went to his junior high school counselor and complained about it. The counselor was aghast and turned the parents in to government authorities. The reason the court gave for its action was that the boy was growing up in what the authorities considered to be an unhealthy environment. The last I heard, the case was going to court in the state of Washington. Hopefully, a ruling will be made in favor of the parents. But they never should have had to go through all of this turmoil, pain, and expense in the first place. You can bet there are hundreds of demons laughing about this one!

Again, you will find demons in the world of politics. But you will also find them living very close to the centers of financial power and those who control money.

> *For love of money is a root of all kinds of evil. Some people, eager, for money, have wandered from the faith and pierced themselves with many griefs.* (1 Timothy 6:10 NIV)

Money has a way of taking over people's hearts and minds, and then they think they don't need God. But when you sweep Him out of your life, you're opening yourself to evil influences, and as the Scripture says, grief will follow. No matter how much money you have, it will never be enough. Have you ever noticed that some people who have a lot of money only want more? They amass such a huge amount of money that they couldn't possibly spend it all in their lifetime, yet they keep striving for more, more, more! No wonder the Bible says the love of money is the root of all kinds of evil.

PRINCIPALITIES

> *For we wrestle not against flesh and blood, but against principalities, against powers, against the rulers of the darkness of this world, against spiritual wickedness in high places.*
> (Ephesians 6:12)

Another area of demonic activity is called principalities. Divisions and duties exist within the demonic realm, and powerful demons are delegated control over specific cities and areas. For example, have you ever wondered why so much homosexual activity happens within the city of San Francisco? If you're a tourist in San Francisco, they'll give you a map that highlights different areas of the city, and included in it are directions to the homosexual neighborhoods. They are actually proud of the sexual perversion that takes place in their city, and they use it as a tourist attraction! But the principality over San Francisco is a demon of homosexuality. As a result, you are going to find all sorts of like-minded demons there, along with all sorts of sexual perversions.

If you are sensitive to such things, and God has given you a great degree of discernment, you can begin to feel the demonic powers that exist within a certain city or area. For example, I would never want to live in New York City because of the spirit of violence there. The city is strongly influenced by demons of violence, murder, and fear, and I would not want to live in a place where I felt those things so strongly. In the same way, I would not want to live in San Francisco because of the controlling spirit of homosexuality and perversion. If God called me there or if I went there to visit, I wouldn't be afraid, because I have the Holy Spirit within me, but it would not be my choice!

If you happen to live in New York or San Francisco, please don't be offended. I'm not equating your city with Sodom or Gomorrah. Every city has its controlling demon, but that doesn't mean the city is entirely sold out to Lucifer. It does mean Lucifer has appointed one of his powerful generals to be in charge of demonic activity within the city—to engage in spiritual warfare against the people who live there.

Some people are attracted to certain cities because of the demonic activity that takes place there. For instance, homosexuals come from all over to settle in San Francisco, because they know they'll be free to indulge in their favorite sin without fear of being exposed or condemned. In the same way, a criminal might be attracted to New York, because there is so much violence there already. He feels he has a pretty good chance of getting away with whatever criminal activity he wants to pursue. Wherever you live, you have to know the controlling demons so you can stand against them. You must know how to pray and strengthen yourself and be aware of the particular demons trying to destroy the people who live in your city.

There are people who think nothing of going to church on Sunday morning, then drinking, carousing, and doing whatever else they want to do during the week. You've heard the old saying— pray like a saint on Sunday morning and live like the devil the rest of the week. I once lived in an area of the United States where a Jezebel spirit—a spirit of rebellion—destroyed some men who could have been great leaders in the kingdom of God. These men had powerful churches and large followings, but when other men began to teach about the importance of faith, they didn't understand it and spoke out against it with great vehemence and passion. They didn't even wait to see if God was involved in what was being said, but they immediately went on the attack. These men fell right into step with the controlling demon of their city. As a result, they opened themselves up to other demonic influences. Some of them got involved in adultery and alcoholism, among other things. Some of them are wandering the streets of a major city today as drunken, helpless bums! It's pathetic, but it's a prime example of what demons can do to a man or woman of God.

You have to know where demons live and the ways in which they will try to attack you. A battle is going on out there, and you're in it whether you realize it or not. Never think you're exempt from demonic attacks! Always keep a watch on yourself.

Stay in constant prayer. Check your thoughts and actions against the Word of God. Don't be fooled into thinking something is OK just because everyone else does it.

Lester Sumrall once told me a story about one of his experiences in Las Vegas. He was called to preach at a particular church, and when the time came to give him the offering, the church treasurer asked him if he wanted his honorarium in money or casino chips. When Brother Sumrall expressed surprise over the question and said that, of course, he didn't want the casino chips, the treasurer told him his experience was that most visiting preachers took the chips. Can you imagine? They would come in and preach about the importance of living a godly life; then they'd be paid in chips so they could go down to the casino and spend their evenings playing roulette and black jack!

Even men and women of God have been seduced. Many Christians believe it's OK to gamble, to see movies filled with sex and violence, and to do anything they want to just because "everyone else is doing it." That attitude makes it so easy to slide into demonic activity before you know what has happened to you.

Again, I remind you that it's important not to give demons too much credit and not to let ourselves spend too much time thinking about them. But at the same time, it's important to know as much about demons as we possibly can—how they operate, where they like to live, and where they come from. The more we understand about demons, the more we will be able to take action against them—and the more we will be able to defeat them.

CHAPTER 4

FOLLOWING JESUS INTO BATTLE

Some people seem to think that the more spiritual you are, the less you'll have to do with demons, but to quote the old song, "It ain't necessarily so." In fact, just the opposite is likely to be true. Usually, the more you strive to follow Jesus, to be like Him, and to reflect His glory, the more encounters you'll have with these creatures from hell. How should you act when you are confronted by demonic power? You should act the same way Jesus Christ did when He came into contact with demons. Jesus is our example and our pattern, and if we truly reflect Him, we will have more, not less, contact with demons for two reasons.

First, the demons will seek us out in an attempt to get us to stop living for God. They don't like Christians, because Christians are going about the business of snatching human souls out of their grip. The demons want to stop you, because as a born-again, Spirit-filled Christian, you are a real threat to them.

Second, as a Christian you are likely to have more open confrontations with demons because God is likely to lead you into situations where confrontation is necessary. It is His power within you that assures your victory over the forces of hell, and

He wants you to use that power to advance His kingdom and set free the captives of Lucifer and his armies.

THE GREAT TEMPTATION

When it comes to preparation for dealing with demons, nothing could serve us better than studying the life of Jesus. Our Savior had many battles with devils throughout His earthly lifetime, beginning very early in His ministry. In fact, the fourth chapter of Matthew tells us that the first thing Jesus did upon the official beginning of His ministry was to go into the wilderness where He was tempted by Satan.

For the first thirty years of His life, Jesus stayed pretty much in the background, with the exception of when He was twelve years old and He confounded the scribes and Pharisees at the temple with His wisdom. But at the age of thirty, He asked His cousin, John the Baptist, to baptize Him.

> *And Jesus, when he was baptized, went up straightway out of the water: and, lo, the heavens were opened unto him, and he saw the Spirit of God descending like a dove, and lighting upon him: and lo a voice from heaven, saying, This is my beloved Son, in whom I am well pleased.*
>
> (Matthew 3:16–17)

This was a significant event, because it was at this time that Jesus received a special anointing of the Holy Spirit, and the focus shifted from John to Jesus. The time had come for Jesus to increase in power and influence. Immediately after His baptism, Jesus went into the wilderness to be tempted by the devil. He fasted for forty days and nights in preparation for the next three years, which would include His death and resurrection.

Before we continue, I need to give you a bit of advice. You should never go on a fast of this length unless God specifically commands it, and even then, you had better be sure you're really hearing from God. A prolonged fast can do tremendous damage to the mind, body, and spirit. I've known people who've undergone such a fast, but instead of coming back with power and anointing, they wound up with goofy ideas and weakness of mind. Ask yourself why you are fasting; because the fact that you can fast for a long period of time does not make you a spiritual giant. I don't mean to be harsh, but this is wisdom we all need.

When Jesus' fast was over, He was hungry. That's probably one of the great understatements of all time. He was more than hungry—He was famished! Satan came to Him saying, in essence, "You poor fellow! I know you must be starved half to death. But listen, if You're really the Son of God, why don't You just turn some of these stones into bread?" Can't you just imagine the "concerned" look on the devil's face?

But Jesus withstood the temptation. Looking His adversary square in the eyes, the Lord replied, *"It is written: 'Man shall not live on bread alone, but on every word that comes from the mouth of God'"* (Matthew 4:4 NIV).

Satan didn't even try to argue with Jesus. He was disarmed with Scripture, and there was nothing he could do but turn his attention elsewhere. Then he took Jesus up to the top of the temple and tried to get Him to jump off. He was like a child saying, "You're supposed to be the Son of God, but I really find it hard to believe. However, if you'll prove it by jumping off the temple and letting your angels carry you safely to the ground below, then I'll really be convinced." This time, Satan himself attempted to use Scripture. (See Psalm 91:12.)

For it is written: "He will command his angels concerning you, and they will lift you up in their hands, so that you will not strike your foot against a stone." (Matthew 4:6 NIV)

Satan was trying to get Jesus to use His power, not for some great purpose but merely to show off, and Jesus wouldn't oblige. Once again, Jesus deflected him with Scripture. *"It is also written: 'Do not put the Lord your God to the test'"* (Matthew 4:7 NIV).

Once again, Satan was defeated. But he wasn't finished yet. He then took Jesus up to a very high mountain and showed Him all the kingdoms of the world. Then he told Jesus he would surrender all these kingdoms to Him if only Jesus would bow down and worship him. Think about what a temptation that must have been. Jesus had come to redeem the world through His death on the cross. He could look into the future and see a time when He was going to be rejected by His friends, savagely beaten by Roman soldiers, and then nailed to a cross and killed. In essence, the devil was saying, "Hey, you don't have to go through all of that. Just bow down and worship me, and I'll give you all these things. You don't have to go through any of that agony!"

However, Jesus knew that if He bowed down to Satan, even for an instant, the war would be over and Satan would win, bringing Almighty God to His knees, which had been his objective all along. But Jesus also knew that those kingdoms were not the devil's to give. Do you ever look around and wonder why people who seem to live such wicked lives do so well in this world? They seem to be so blessed with their beautiful homes, fancy cars, and more money in the bank than they know what to do with. From all appearances, it looks like selling out to Satan has paid off. Someone who didn't know any better might think, *If that's how Satan treats his people, then I'm all for him.*

But all of those things are only temporary. They will not last, and when they come crashing down, the fall thereof will be mighty indeed! Furthermore, there will be a terrible price to pay for not receiving Jesus as your Lord and Savior. Jesus would not bow before Satan, and neither should you.

After failing three times, Satan gave up. The Bible says the devil left Jesus, and the angels came and ministered to Him. (See Matthew 4:11.)

THE TOOLS OF BATTLE

To be a successful devil-fighter, you must hit the devil and his demons right in the face with the Scriptures. Give them chapter and verse from the Word of God. That's something they can't withstand, and it's something they can't fight. In order to come against the enemy with the Word of God, you have to *know* the Word of God. This comes from spending time reading it, meditating on it, digesting it, and memorizing it. If you know what God has to say about things, then you are more apt to recognize the tricks of the enemy.

Don't think for a moment that demons don't know the Bible. They know it very well. They know it better then some Christians do! Satan and his followers regularly twist Scripture to convince people that the Word of God says something it doesn't really say. Again, the only way to combat that is to know the Bible for yourself so you won't be fooled when Satan tries to take an isolated verse out of context and twist it out of shape.

An example of this is the controversial religious group called The Family. They used to be known as The Children of God, and they consider themselves Christians. But they have totally twisted Jesus' words about love. Somewhere along the line, these people began to confuse sex with love. They have gone so far as to teach their followers that they should attempt to use sex to bring others into God's kingdom. They have taught their young girls to use their bodies as a means of evangelism. Can you imagine anything so perverse, so far from the true teachings of Scripture? Yet that is the sort of thing that can happen when people listen to Satan's twisting of the Word of God.

> *Submit yourselves therefore to God. Resist the devil, and he will flee from you.* (James 4:7)

Satan left Jesus after tempting Him to sin three times and failing each time. But know this, when Satan retreats, it's never for good. He only retreats far enough and long enough to plan the next series of attacks in his battle for your soul. Don't ever think you can let your guard down, because the moment you do, he'll be waiting to pounce like a roaring lion. We always have to be ready—always on our guard.

Jesus knew He hadn't seen the last of the devil or his foot soldiers:

> *While they were going out, a man who was demon-possessed and could not talk was brought to Jesus. And when the demon was driven out, the man who had been mute spoke. The crowd was amazed and said, "Nothing like this has ever, been seen in Israel."* (Matthew 9:32–33 NIV)

I have had encounters with this type of demon. Sometimes, the person with such a devil cannot speak at all, and other times, he is kept from speaking at particular times. I have seen occasions when demon-possessed people got into a prayer line but then couldn't tell me what they wanted or needed. I would ask what the problem was, and they would just stand there staring at me. When I looked into their eyes, I saw the wheels were turning. They wanted to say something but just couldn't. If you're listening to the Holy Spirit, it's fairly easy to see in situations such as this that a demon is involved. But once you've cast out the demon in the name of Jesus, the problem is solved.

ACCUSATIONS

But the Pharisees said, "It is by the prince of demons that he drives out demons."   (Matthew 9:34 NIV)

The Pharisees had a typical reaction to what Jesus was doing. They thought He was able to cast out devils only because He was in league with the prince of demons. They thought He was a devil Himself. People haven't really changed very much over the last two thousand years. When God first showed me He wanted me involved in the business of setting people free from demons, a lot of people didn't like the idea. They were embarrassed by it, because the process of casting demons out can be noisy, messy, and disturbing. They wanted me to have nice, quiet, uneventful church services. But so many people were in bondage, and I wasn't going to just walk away from them. Besides, the Lord had said, "Do it," so I really didn't have any choice in the matter.

Some people were so upset by what I was doing that they said the same thing the Pharisees said about Jesus in Matthew 9:34— that I was possessed by demons. My answer to them was, "All right, if I have demons, help me get rid of them. Cast them out of me." I didn't have any takers.

In Matthew 12:22, Jesus experienced another encounter with demons and Pharisees. This time a demon-possessed man who was both blind and mute was brought to Jesus. Once again, He cast out the demon, and the man was healed of his infirmities. The ordinary people were so impressed that they began to wonder out loud if Jesus might not be the long-awaited Messiah. But not the

Pharisees! Once more, their astute conclusion was that Jesus was in league with Beelzebub, another name for Satan. Jesus reminded the Pharisees in verse 25 that a *"house divided against itself shall not stand."* If Satan himself was going around casting demons out of people, then we could just sit back and watch his evil kingdom fall apart.

Are people benefited by a ministry of deliverance? Absolutely! Lives are changed dramatically. Alcoholics and drug addicts are instantly set free as demons are driven out. People find deliverance from things that have plagued them for years. Satan never does anything to help anyone, so he can't be responsible for the casting out of demons.

If you are prepared to fight demons, you should also be prepared to deal with the slanderous accusations some people are going to toss at you. Some people won't understand and will accuse you of all sorts of things—I guarantee it.

ANOINTING

In my experience, the anointing of the Holy Spirit for deliverance is a stronger, rougher, more militant anointing than the anointing for healing. It is an anointing that will put you immediately into combat situations. Make no mistake about it—deliverance is war! Some people would like to pretend we're not at war, but we are.

I have prayed for people who have been in demonic bondage for ten or fifteen years, and when deliverance began to take place, they would shake and jerk uncontrollably. Their pastor would look on and think, *I've prayed for you before. Why didn't you jump like that when I prayed?* The fact is, that pastor didn't ask God for a deliverance anointing. Perhaps he even sought not to receive such an anointing, because he didn't want to look foolish. If you want to see people set free, you can't worry about things like your appearance!

Jesus didn't worry about His dignity, and He was the Son of God. If He had worried about such things, He never would have allowed Himself to be born in a manger. He never would have associated with the likes of prostitutes and tax collectors. But He got right down there in the dirt, so to speak, because He knew the hurting people were there, the ones who needed His help.

AUTHORITY

A Canaanite woman from that vicinity came to him, crying out, "Lord, Son of David, have mercy on me! My daughter is demon-possessed and suffering terribly." Jesus did not answer a word. So his disciples came to him and urged him, "Send her, away for she keeps crying out after us." He answered, "I was sent only to the lost sheep of Israel." The woman came and knelt before him. "Lord, help me!" she said. He replied, "It is not right to take the children's bread and toss it to the dogs." "Yes it is, Lord," she said. "Even the dogs eat the crumbs that fall from their masters' table." Then Jesus said to her, "Woman, you have great faith! Your request is granted." And her daughter was healed at that moment.

(Matthew 15:22–28 NIV)

The Scriptures don't tell us how old this woman's daughter was, but based on my own experience, I wouldn't be surprised if she was no more than seven or eight years old, perhaps even younger. You see, parents are responsible for bringing deliverance and help to their children. If you don't keep authority over your children and teach them how to live for the Lord while they're growing up, demons will come in and live with them. That's why we read stories in our newspapers of twelve- and thirteen-year-olds shooting their parents or neighbors and never showing the least bit of remorse.

One afternoon, I flipped on the television and caught a few minutes of a popular talk show. On this particular show, they featured children who had given their parents all kinds of grief. The parents, with their children, were talking about all of the terrible things they had been through. Now some of the people in the studio audience were quick to blame the parents for their children's misbehavior, saying things like, "If you had disciplined them once in a while, this wouldn't have happened."

One of the mothers in particular became very angry over such allegations. "You don't know how many times I corrected my child," she said, "How many times I punished him and spanked him and did everything I could think of to change his behavior, but he still wouldn't change."

I have no doubt she was telling the truth. But you see, she didn't know anything about *divine correction*. It was obvious to me that some of the children featured on that show did what they did because they had evil spirits living within them, and an evil spirit cannot be hurt by a spanking. When demons cause children to do things that will get them into trouble, those children may not even remember afterward what they did. But when it comes time for the spanking to be administered, the spirit is somewhere laughing, and the children are left to suffer the pain. That only causes the children to suffer even further damage. What the children on that talk show needed was someone to minister to them in the name of Jesus, someone to take authority over the evil spirits in their lives and cast them out.

We read a lot these days about child abuse, and I think it's a terrible problem in our society. But much of the time, it is brought about by demons that get inside of children and then torture and torment the parents until they totally lose their tempers and end up battering an innocent child. It is also true that child abuse is often caused by demons of rage, anger, and bitterness that have taken residence in the parents. I don't want to imply that all cases of child abuse are the result of the work of evil spirits. Some people are just plain guilty of being mean and abusive to their children, but there are many instances when demons are involved.

Sometimes people ask me, "Do you really think a little child can be indwelt by an evil spirit?"

Yes I do. I believe it because I've seen it with my own eyes, and it can be a remarkable thing to see. Little boys come for prayer in their little suits, having their hair neatly combed and looking like perfect little gentlemen. Little girls come with bows in their hair, wearing their pretty dresses and looking like little porcelain dolls. But when I lay hands on them, they begin to growl, moan, and jerk as the demons fight to stay in them. Parents, your innocent, sweet children are not immune to demonic attack. I'm not telling you this to scare you. I'm telling you because it's something you need to know.

I specifically remember one case in Minneapolis when a woman called and asked if she could bring her daughter in for prayer. She explained to me that the girl sometimes became violent, would beat her mother with her fists, and would throw things at her. I figured we were probably talking about a teenager, so I was surprised when the mother showed up with a little girl who couldn't have been more than ten years old.

They came to a Sunday morning service when I was preaching, and I immediately knew who they were. The little girl was nervous and fidgety throughout the service, but it was not the normal type of energy one might associate with children. She was up and down, up and down, and left to go to the bathroom several times during the course of the service. Her mother finally brought her to the altar for prayer. As I laid hands on her, she immediately began to scream and kick. The ushers came running to help me, but they were too late—I had already received a vicious kick in the shin!

Once we had control of the situation, I was able to take authority over the demons in that little girl and cast them out of her by the power and name of Jesus. When she left the church that morning, she was smiling, happy, and acting like the sweetest little girl you ever saw. The difference was amazing. That's what the Lord had done for her.

If you want to be involved in a ministry of deliverance, you will undoubtedly come across situations such as the one I have just described. Never let a child go away from you still in bondage. But at the same time, parents must keep divine authority over their children so the demons do not come back once they have been driven out.

Another thing to learn from this story about the Canaanite woman is that deliverance is part of the "children's bread." It's a basic part of the gospel. I've heard people say, "I'm not into deliverance." If you're not into deliverance, then you're not into the basics of the gospel. Bringing deliverance to the captives should be one of the primary tenets of the Christian faith. Everyone in your church should be taught how to cast out devils—from your children to your oldest member.

> *For unclean spirits, crying with a loud voice, came out of many that were possessed with them: and many taken with palsies, and that were lame, were healed.* (Acts 8:7)

I have been asked why demons sometimes cry out as they are being forced to leave the human body they've inhabited. It is because they're afraid of the authority being used against them. They don't want to go, and they know the destruction that awaits them.

CONTROL THROUGH JESUS

They went to Capernaum, and when the Sabbath came, Jesus went into the synagogue and began to teach. The people were amazed at his teaching, because he taught them as one who had authority, not as the teachers of the law. Just then a man in their synagogue who was possessed by an impure spirit cried out, "What do you want with us, Jesus of Nazareth? Have you come to destroy us? I know who you are—the Holy One of God!" "Be quiet!" said Jesus sternly. "Come out of him!" The impure spirit shook the man violently and came out of him with a shriek. (Mark 1:21–26 NIV)

Picture this scene as if it had happened today. This man is sitting in church, his arm draped around his pretty wife, and his two adorable kids are sitting next to him. All of a sudden, he begins to scream out, "Leave us alone, Jesus! Leave us alone!" I mean, right in the middle of the sermon he starts hollering like a stuck pig. It probably scared his wife half to death, along with the rest of the people.

What did Jesus do in this situation? Did He summon the ushers and tell them to escort the gentleman outside because he was disrupting the service? No, Jesus simply ordered the demon to come out of the man, and the demon obeyed. Jesus took authority over the situation, cast the demon out with a few simple words, and went on with His sermon.

Notice that Jesus maintained control. He didn't let the demon put on a big show and distract everyone's attention from worshipping God. He dealt with things directly and as simply as possible, and that's the way we are to do it as we follow Him. At times demon-possessed people will yell, kick, and struggle, but we still must deal with them as quickly as possible, especially if they are doing all of those things in the middle of the church service. Then we can get on with what we've come together for, which is to worship God and learn from His Word.

Another thing I want you to see is that demons will react to the presence of God. This demon was prompted to show itself by the authority of Jesus, and as we are representatives of Jesus, full of the Holy Spirit, demons may also begin to manifest themselves in our presence. For example, I used to live in Southern California, not too far from a place crawling with demons of all types. I'm talking about Hollywood in general and the Sunset Strip in particular. Any born-again, Spirit-filled Christian who walks down the Sunset Strip after dark is going to see demons manifesting themselves. You'll see some people glaring at you for no reason and others hurrying away from you. Some people might yell at you. They won't know why, but it's because they have demons in them, and those demons are reacting to the presence and authority of the Spirit of God in you.

One thing that made some people angry with me a few years ago was that they would come to my meetings and the deliverance anointing would be so strong that demons would begin to manifest all over the room. Some people said I was working the people into a frenzy or getting them to act like they were being delivered. But that wasn't it at all. What was happening was that the authority was there, and the demons couldn't stand it and began to show themselves.

Don't ever think for a moment that just because someone is sitting in church, that person can't be demonized. Sometimes the safest place for a demon to hide is in church. Too many churches don't believe in the ministry of deliverance. Some don't even believe in the existence of demons, and you can't set someone free from something you don't believe in. What they're doing is telling those who are troubled by demons, "I'm sorry, but I can't help you, because I don't think you really have a problem." What a tragedy!

I have no doubt that if pastors throughout America would study what the Scriptures have to say about deliverance, they would ask God to give them the anointing for deliverance, and one of the greatest revivals of all time would sweep through this nation.

PREPARE TO WIN

A man in the crowd answered, "Teacher, I brought you my son, who is possessed by a spirit that has robbed him of speech. Whenever it seizes him, it throws him to the ground. He foams at the mouth, gnashes his teeth and becomes rigid. I asked your disciples to drive out the spirit, but they could not." "You unbelieving generation," Jesus replied, "how long shall I stay with you? How long shall I put up with you? Bring the boy to me." So they brought him. When the spirit saw Jesus, it immediately threw the boy into a convulsion. He fell to the ground and rolled around, foaming at the mouth...When Jesus saw that a crowd was running to the scene, he rebuked the impure spirit, "You deaf and mute spirit," he said, "I command you, come out of him and never enter him again."

(Mark 9:17–20, 25 NIV)

This story took place as Jesus, Peter, James, and John were coming down from the mountain, after His transfiguration, to meet the other nine apostles. This demon-possessed boy had been brought to the apostles for deliverance, but they couldn't deliver him from this tormenting demon. The boy had been troubled by this spirit since early childhood. Imagine the terror and suffering this poor boy and his family had been through. Sometimes the spirit would throw the boy into water and at other times into fire. The destructive rage of this demon was so violent that its behavior severely injured its human host, determined to kill him.

The foaming at the mouth is a pretty good depiction of the manifestation you might expect when someone is in the control of an evil spirit. Based on what I've observed, I would say this is one of the best descriptions of demon-controlled behavior in the entire Bible. This is so typical of the sort of behavior you'll encounter when you're dealing with demons. It can be frightening at first, but God will give you the courage and the strength to go on. Sometimes my natural mind wants to run away from it all, but my spirit is so tuned in to God that it keeps me in there until the job is finished and the demon has gone.

When Jesus rebuked the evil spirit, you can imagine how the nine apostles felt. They must have been ashamed and embarrassed, because they had not been able to do a thing for this poor little boy. They tried to cast the demon out of him, but it had, in essence, just laughed at them. "Sorry, folks you can try all you want, but I'm staying right here."

But when Jesus came around, the demon was immediately subject to His authority, and the boy was instantly healed. The apostles wanted to know what they had been doing wrong. Why had the demon refused to obey them? Jesus told them this kind could only come out by prayer and fasting. (See Mark 9:29.)

There are times when you really have to prepare yourself for battle. Now I believe that as a Christian you should be prepared to do spiritual battle every day of your life. You should be spending much time praying, reading your Bible, meditating on God's Word, and fellowshipping with other Christians. All of these things will help to keep you strong spiritually. But at the same time, certain situations may require extra effort on your part. For example, you may need to pray and fast to prepare for a particular conflict or situation.

How will you know when special preparation is required? God will tell you. If you are listening to Him and in tune with the Holy

Spirit, you will know what God is saying to you and will be ready for anything that comes along. That is why it is so important to spend as much time in prayer as you possibly can, listening to Him and finding out what He wants to say to you. As you read through the Gospels, you will find that Jesus prayed a great deal. Many times He went up onto a mountain or got away to some other isolated place where He could be alone with His heavenly Father and pray all night. You can know for a fact that Jesus didn't just talk all night long. He was listening, enjoying His Father's presence, and communing as friend with friend.

Have you ever been in an uncomfortable silence? Perhaps you're with someone you really don't know all that well; you don't know what to talk to them about, and an awkward silence creeps in. You're fumbling around in your mind, trying to think of something interesting to say, but it's really difficult. On the other hand, there is the type of deep silence that develops between friends. You can be with someone you truly love, and not a word passes between you, but that's OK because there is an unspoken communication. You can just be silent together and love one another. That is the sort of relationship we all need to develop with our heavenly Father. We need to learn to enjoy just sitting with Him, resting with Him, and being ministered to by the joy and peace of the Holy Spirit.

Being in His presence is one of the greatest experiences imaginable. It is a source of strength, wisdom, peace, and joy. It is a means of preparation for the battles Christians have to face in this world. Jesus spent countless hours with His Father to help prepare Him for all the battles He faced, right up till and including His death at the hands of Roman soldiers. You simply cannot stand against the forces of hell without being properly prepared.

During the course of my ministry, I have come face-to-face with all sorts of demonic forces and manifestations. I have seen people foam at the mouth, and I have heard them growl. I have seen them slither across the floor and fall down as if they were dead. I've even observed people barking like they were dogs. But I've never been stopped in my tracks. I have never recoiled in surprise or shock, because I have always been ready and willing to be used of God in any way.

Sometimes when a demon is being cast out of a person, it's so strong that you can see a knot coming up through the body. I've actually felt the demonic presence moving through the person's body as I prayed for them. I have also seen instances when the people being set free were left so weak from the great battle taking place within their bodies and the major force being wrenched out of them that they had to go to bed for awhile. One time a man I was praying for was actually injured by the force of the demon leaving him, and he began to bleed around his mouth.

Why am I telling you all this? To help you prepare for battle so that you will not be taken off guard by the enemy's tactics. This is a war we must win, and in order to win it, we have to be prepared for everything the enemy throws at us.

> *Finally, be strong in the Lord and in his mighty power. Put on the full armor of God so that you can take your stand against the devil's schemes.* (Ephesians 6:10–11 NIV)

Paul doesn't say, "Be weak and confused and have small faith"! No! God has called us to a position of authority and active opposition to the schemes of evil spirits.

CHAPTER 5

THE GATES OF HELL WILL NOT PREVAIL

And I say also unto thee, That thou art Peter, and upon this rock I will build my church; and the gates of hell shall not prevail against it. (Matthew 16:18)

Some people misunderstand this verse. They turn it around and look at it as if Jesus was saying the church would be able to prevail against the forces of hell. In other words, they have a fortress mentality where the church is standing strong and secure despite an all-out assault against it by the armies of Satan. But that's not the picture Jesus was giving us. The church is to be on the *offensive* against the forces of evil. When I think about this, I see in my mind a bunch of people with a battering ram actually crashing down the gates of hell and releasing those who are held prisoner there. *We are to be the ones who are on the offensive.* We are to put demons to flight, and not the other way around. That's the way it was in the church of the first century, and that's the way it ought to be today!

In the book of Acts, we find that the early church was still doing battle with demonic powers, even after the resurrection of

Jesus and after the Holy Spirit was given on the day of Pentecost. This is important, because many Christians believe all demons were utterly destroyed by Jesus' resurrection. They were defeated, but they were not destroyed. There is a difference. They will be destroyed when Jesus returns to set up His kingdom here on earth. Others believe that when the Holy Spirit came in His fullness on Pentecost, demonic power was swept away from this planet. But that is also an erroneous belief.

People have actually told me that there couldn't possibly have been a manifestation of demons following Jesus' atoning work on the cross. But anyone who says that obviously hasn't carefully read through the book of Acts! Nor have they looked around them to see what's going on in the world today.

The first century church had to deal with demons, and we can expect to deal with demons today, too. As long as we live on this earth, Satan will be out to destroy us.

FACING SATAN HEAD-ON

They traveled through the whole island until they came to Paphos. There they met a Jewish sorcerer and false prophet named Bar-Jesus, who was an attendant of the proconsul, Sergius Paulus. The proconsul, an intelligent man, sent for Barnabas and Saul because he wanted to hear the word of God. But Elymas the sorcerer (for that is what his name means) opposed them and tried to turn the proconsul from the faith. Then Saul, who was also called Paul, filled with the Holy Spirit, looked straight at Elymas and said, "You are a child of the devil and an enemy of everything that is right! You are full of all kinds of deceit and trickery. Will you never stop perverting the right ways of the Lord? Now the hand of the Lord is

*against you. You are going to be blind for a time, not even able
to see the light of the sun."* (Acts 13:6–11 NIV)

It happened just like Paul said it would. Immediately, Elymas
was unable to see. As a sorcerer, Elymas was undoubtedly in league
with all sorts of hellish influences and was well-acquainted with
demons. This was an encounter with evil spirits, even though the
Scriptures don't specifically say it.

Notice that Paul looked straight at Elymas. The King James
Version says he set his eyes on him; I think that was a divine activity. At that moment, Paul looked at Elymas with the eyes of discernment and saw all the evil, deceit, and mischief in him. Being
full of the Holy Spirit, Paul was not acting in his own power, but
in the power and might of God. Paul confronted the enemy and
called him what he was—an enemy of everything that is right.
Like Paul, we must be yielded to God, and we must learn to operate in the discernment, power, and anointing of the Holy Spirit.

Are you full of the Holy Spirit? If you aren't, you need to be.
You need to surrender to Him and ask Him to fill you, empower
you, and give you all the gifts He has for you.

FREEDOM IS A CHOICE

This encounter between Paul and Elymas raises an important question. Undoubtedly, this sorcerer had a demon or demons
within him, so why didn't Paul cast them out? Why did he blast
the man instead of dealing with the demons? Paul did this because
Elymas was totally open to the demons in his life. He wanted them
to be there, and he even used them to earn his livelihood as a sorcerer. People like that exist today, too. They don't want to be set
free. They have sold out to the devil. They haven't been invaded by
demons; they have taken them in willingly and don't want to get

rid of them. There can be no deliverance for those who do not want to be delivered.

By contrast, consider this story:

> *Once when we were going to the place of prayer, we were met by a female slave who had a spirit by which she predicted the future. She earned a great deal of money for her owners by fortune-telling. She followed Paul and the rest of us, shouting, "These men are servants of the Most High God, who are telling you the way to be saved." She kept this up for many days. Finally Paul became so annoyed that he turned around and said to the spirit, "In the name of Jesus Christ I command you to come out of her!" At that moment the spirit left her. When her owners realized that their hope of making money was gone, they seized Paul and Silas and dragged them into the marketplace to face the authorities.*
>
> (Acts 16:16–19 NIV)

Once again, the demon recognized the authority of the gospel. It knew who Paul and Silas were and openly admitted it. Everything this girl was saying was true, but it began to annoy Paul because she just wouldn't shut up. Everywhere he went, she was right behind him shouting these things. Instead of attracting people to hear what he had to say, it began to have the opposite effect. Besides that, Paul could feel in his spirit that something was wrong. Something about her actions was evil even though the words were true. Finally, Paul had had enough, and he commanded the evil spirit to come out of her.

Was everyone happy that this poor girl who had been in bondage for so long had been set free? Not at all! In fact, just the opposite was true. The girl was a slave, and her owners had made quite a bit of money through her telling people's fortunes. They realized right away that they had lost their meal ticket, and they weren't very happy about it. In fact, they got the whole town riled up against Paul and Silas, so much so that the local magistrates sentenced them to be beaten with rods. Then, after they had been severely beaten, they were thrown into prison, and the jailer was commanded to keep them locked up securely.

Isn't that crazy? Wouldn't you think the townspeople would look at this girl, see her smiling, happy, and free from demonic possession, and beg Paul and Silas to pray for them? Wouldn't you think they'd say, "We see what you've done for this poor girl, now won't you please do the same for us?" But a mob mentality took over. People were frightened by what had happened, and they didn't like outsiders coming in and messing up the status quo. The result was trouble for Paul and Silas.

Don't ever think the world will be on your side if you're battling against the forces of hell. Many times the world will fight you just as hard as the demons do. But even here, God was able to use the situation for good. The rest of the chapter tells us how God miraculously set Paul and Silas free and used the incident to bring about the salvation of the jailer and his entire household.

CAST DOWN BY REPUTATION

In Acts 19, we find a rather humorous story about the seven sons of Sceva, a Jewish chief priest, who were going around trying to cast out evil spirits in the name of Jesus. But they didn't really know Jesus at all—not to mention the fact that they had never made Jesus their Lord and Savior and been born again. These fellows had apparently seen Paul casting out demons in the name of Jesus, and they decided they'd do the same thing. They came to a man who was possessed with a particularly violent spirit and commanded that spirit to come out of him, *in the name of Jesus whom Paul preaches*" (Acts 19:13 NIV).

They attempted to use the name of the Lord like it was some sort of lucky charm, and it isn't. They might as well have been saying "hocus pocus" instead of "in the name of Jesus." Yes, there is power and might in the name of Jesus, but only for those who are truly born again. The name of Jesus is not to be trifled with. It is not a toy or a magic charm.

The Bible says the man with the demon replied, *"Jesus I know, and Paul I know about, but who are you?"* (Acts 19:15 NIV). Then the man with the evil spirit jumped on them, tearing at their clothes and beating them so severely that *"they ran out of the house naked and bleeding"* (verse 16). It's funny to think of those men running down the road as fast as they could and thinking, *We sure won't try that again!*

Lester Sumrall was someone I particularly admired because he was not afraid of the truth. He told it the way it was, no matter what anyone else thought, and he saw hundreds of people set free from enslavement by demons. I have heard him talk about the time when he was driving a demon out of a man, and the demon spoke to him and said, "I know who you are. We've heard of you."

Have demons heard of you? If you are living for God, you can bet they've heard of you, because you are a threat to them. If you are aware of their existence, and if you are willing to take them on with the power and might of Jesus, they've heard of you because they are afraid of you! I think it would be a great thing to hear from the mouth of a demon, "I know who you are. You're the one who beats us everywhere we go. You're the one who has destroyed so many of us!" That's the way it can and should be for you. But you have to know where your authority lies. You can't take it lightly. It isn't a game to go up against the worst that hell has to offer. Considering that, those men who were beaten by the demon-possessed man were actually lucky to escape with their lives. They were embarrassed and bruised, but at least they were still living and breathing!

WHAT ARE WE UP AGAINST?

Finally, my brethren, be strong in the Lord, and in the power of his might. Put on the whole armor of God, that ye may be able to stand against the wiles of the devil. For we wrestle not against flesh and blood, but against principalities, against powers, against the rulers of the darkness of this world, against spiritual wickedness in high places. (Ephesians 6:10–12)

Notice all the times the word *against* is used. The question is, just exactly what are we going up against? First of all, Paul makes it clear we are not fighting against flesh and blood. Something more than human strength is at work here; this is a supernatural battle. We are wrestling against principalities. That means we are going up against the rulers of evil—princes who have been set up to reign over territories, regions, and cities. We are not to stand aside and let these wicked beings take over our communities. We are to stand up and do battle against them!

Second, we are coming against powers. Evil powers are at loose in this world, and we are called to stand against them. Third, we are standing against the rulers of the darkness of this age. We are against the darkness and for the light. In fact, Jesus calls us to be the light of the world. (See Matthew 5:14.) We are to walk in the light and bring others into the light. At times you might start talking to a person, perhaps to share Jesus with that person, and you can sense something is wrong. That person is ensnared by darkness and needs to be brought into the light. Fourth, we also wrestle against spiritual hosts of wickedness in the heavenly places. Paul was referring to the heaven where spirits dwell. *The Living Bible* says we are wrestling *"against huge numbers of wicked spirits in the spirit world"* (Ephesians 6:12).

Vast numbers of demons exist in this universe, but if you have the power of God within you, all of the forces of hell are no match for you. You could be out in the middle of the sea in a little rowboat, surrounded by all of Satan's battleships. He could have every one of his huge guns pointed at you. He could be sending his bombers and his fighter planes over your head. They could be bombing you and strafing you with machine-gun fire—doing everything in the world to destroy you. But as long as you have the Holy Spirit with you in that little boat, the devil's forces won't even be able to mess up your hair!

Praise God for His power and might and for the fact that He lets that power and might flow through His children.

Therefore submit to God. Resist the devil and he will flee from you. (James 4:7 NKJV)

Here are two important ways every believer can obtain power over the devil and his armies. First, be submitted to God. If you are yielded to Him, you will live under His protecting arm, and the devil will have a dickens of a time trying to get through to you! Active, strong resistance is the second way to defeat old Satan. When he comes at you and tries to get you to do something you know you shouldn't do, simply say, "No!" Tell him, "I refuse to listen to you, and I won't do what you want me to do. In Jesus' name, I break your power."

How much better off would this world—and the church—be if people would simply learn to resist the devil? Unfortunately, some people sit around and think about temptation. They ponder what might happen if they just did this one little thing. And before they know what hit them, they're involved in some full-blown sin, and they're wide open for an army of demons to take up residence in them. The simplest way to defeat the devil is just to say *no* to him in the name of Jesus. Unfortunately, some people have never resisted a temptation in their lives! If you start to resist temptation on a consistent basis, you will begin to build up resistance, and you will find it easier and easier to overcome the enemy's temptations. What's more, his temptations will come less and less frequently!

I will say this more than once, because it is the truth: You have been given all power and authority to deal with demons through Jesus Christ. Paul and Silas didn't have anything we don't have. Jesus said the works He did we would do—and greater. (See John 14:12.) In other words, you can be strong in the power of the Lord. You can resist the devil, and you can live in divine freedom!

CHAPTER 6

SEVEN STEPS TO DEMON POSSESSION

Some people invite demons into their lives by getting involved in witchcraft, magic, or New Age activities, and they willingly yield themselves to Satan and his demons. They draw chalk outlines of pentagrams on the floor, say strange incantations, and flat-out give themselves over to demon control. Other people invite demons into their lives in a less blatant way. They get involved in things such as drinking, taking drugs, and promiscuous sexual activity, and because of the lifestyle they've chosen, they wind up with a host of demons taking up residence in their bodies. Then there are others who become entrapped by demons through the seven steps I want to talk about in this chapter—Regression, Repression, Suppression, Depression, Oppression, Regression, Obsession, and Possession. The definitions that follow are my own.

REGRESSION

By *regress*, I mean "to withdraw, to decrease, or backslide." It also means "to revert to a former level, to reverse a trend, or to shift to a lower state." If you are regressing, you are moving backward. A person who is regressing is likely to be a lukewarm Christian. He or she is one of those about whom Jesus said He would spit them out of His mouth. (See Revelation 3:16.)

Such people might follow a path something like this: They were making spiritual progress—reading their Bible, praying, and spending time with the Lord. But one day, they were too tired to study the Bible. They didn't bother to pray the next day, either, and before they realized it, they weren't spending any time at all with God. They soon began to lose what progress they had made, and their spiritual muscles began to atrophy and turn to flab. Thus, they became easy pickings for demonic power.

To understand *regression*, we need to take a look at the opposite word—*progression*. If you are not moving forward, you are probably moving backward. If you're not progressing, you are probably regressing.

Look around at some of the so-called mainline Christian churches, which were formed in the fires of revival. Some of them were birthed as a reaction to the corruption in the church at that time. Sound doctrine had been perverted, and the gospel was not being preached, so brave men put their lives on the line in order to change things. At that time, the Spirit of God burned brightly in those churches. But today many of these churches are spiritually dead. They have become social clubs where most of the people don't even remember why they get together on Sunday morning. What happened? Somewhere along the line they quit progressing and began regressing, eventually to find themselves in a sad condition.

When the communists took over Russia, they did a terrible thing by closing down some of the churches and turning them into museums. Some churches here in America are really nothing more than museums. They're not useful for anything except perhaps the beauty of their stained-glass windows or their ornate furniture. Regression is the first avenue by which Satan takes over any human soul, church, or ministry.

One time when I was having lunch with Lester Sumrall, he said, "I live a progressive life."

I said, "Yes, Sir," which is pretty much all you ever said when Brother Sumrall was talking to you.

"You know," he went on, "a lot of my friends are old and in their rocking chairs now. We started out in ministry about the same time. But I'm still going strong, and they're totally in a regressive state of living."

"Yes, Sir," I said again. It was the truth.

And then he said, "And I want that in you."

"Great!" I said "Give it to me!"

He laughed. "Well, it doesn't quite come like that. It comes by decisions you make. And it comes as a result of how you deal with the challenges of life and the demonic attacks on you." He went on to explain the difference between regression and progression this way: "To regress in the human personality is to go backward in spiritual force and power. The human person is built for a progressive life, an advancing life, and an understanding life."

He told me he kept on the move because he wanted to be progressive. He had made the decision about how he was going to live. "I'm not going to retire. I'm going to leave when it's time."

Regressive people may start to retire years before it's actually time. They give up their goals, relax, and just sort of fade away. General Douglas MacArthur said, "Old soldiers never die; they just fade away." But there is no *fading away* in the kingdom of God. When the righteous grow old, their days get brighter and brighter, not dimmer and dimmer. This is important, because it is the very first way Satan is able to make inroads into the human soul.

*Now the Lord is the Spirit; and where the Spirit of the Lord
is, there is liberty. But we all, with unveiled face, beholding as
in a mirror, the glory of the Lord, are being transformed into
the same image from glory to glory, just as by the Spirit of the
Lord.*   (2 Corinthians 3:17–18 NKJV)

In order to make progress, we need to have liberty. Where
there is liberty, we can feel free to release ourselves to the presence of God and let His Spirit minister to us. But some churches
are so fossilized that every Sunday service is the same. There is
no liberty, and the Spirit has been quenched. It's important to do
things decently and in order and to have a plan to follow, but sometimes the Holy Spirit wants you to discard your plan, because He
has something else in mind. It's important to have the freedom to
follow wherever the Lord wants to lead you. Such liberty brings
progression. A lack of liberty brings regression.

I love the part about being transformed from *"glory to glory."*
In other words, it may be glorious right now, but just you wait,
because it's going to be even more glorious later on. Don't ever
think you've reached the summit. If you reach the point where
you think you have it made or that God has given you everything
He has to give you, that's the day you stop striving to move forward and the day you start sliding back down the hill. Don't ever
stop hungering and thirsting after righteousness. Don't ever stop
wanting more of God or of His Holy Spirit. He has so much to
show us and teach us that it is totally ridiculous for any of us to
think we've gotten to the point that we don't need anything else
from Him.

Another thing about progressive people is that they are interested in others. They are outgoing in the sense that they are willing to give of themselves, and they want to get to know people.
Regressive people are likely to retreat into their own little corner
of the world. They are so preoccupied with themselves that they

can't show interest in anyone else. Which of these types of people do you suppose will be a greater influence for the kingdom of God? Which will be attractive to people and be able to show them the way to Jesus? Progressive people will. If you want to be a blessing to people and lead them to Jesus, you have to have an adventurous, progressive attitude.

Here are four ways to know if you are falling into a pattern of regression.

1. The things that used to bring you excitement and joy no longer do.

You used to be excited when new people came into your church, but now it doesn't make you feel that way. You used to find excitement in reading the Scriptures—as if God was speaking directly to you. But now you have to struggle to keep your mind on what you're reading. You used to love to go to church. You couldn't wait for the Sunday morning service, but now it's a chore to get yourself out of bed. When you sense these things happening in your life, it's time for you to turn your heart toward God. Ask Him to restore to you your first love. Tell Him you're sorry for coldness, and ask Him to give you back your passion.

2. You become careless about your commitment to Jesus and your desire to build God's kingdom.

I have met with young ministers who are just bubbling with excitement over all the things they want to do for God and the furthering of His kingdom. When I meet the same people a year later, they have totally forgotten those goals. They have gotten so busy with the smaller matters that they have forgotten all about the larger matters. They got careless. They adopted the attitude, "If I don't do it, someone else will." That's a regressive attitude. It's the beginning of a long slide downhill.

3. You see your own excuses as more powerful than your faith.

If you have faith in God, you can come through any challenge set before you. Something may look impossible, but you know all things are possible with God. (See Philippians 4:13.) You just keep moving right through that stone mountain if you have to.

But when you begin to regress, you think, *I'll never be able to do that! Who do I think I am to be able to get that done?* Then you start making excuses: *I'm too old,* or *I'm too poor,* or *I'm too young in the faith.* When your excuses have become the size of giants and you need a microscope to examine your faith, then you have really fallen into a regressive state of mind.

4. You are ruled more by your feelings than by making decisions and sticking with them.

If you have failed in your commitment to do something simply because you didn't feel like doing it, you are regressing. However, whether you feel like it or not, if you keep pushing forward because you've made a decision to do something, then you are progressing.

The following are the three characteristics of a progressive person:

1. Progressive people are willing to change.

Progressive people are not tied to the old ways of doing things. They are free to follow the Holy Spirit wherever He may lead. That willingness to change may include changing the way they look at the Word of God. They may find, as they continue to study the Word, that they need to change their thinking on a few points. Some people won't do that. You can sit there and show them clearly that they have erroneous thinking about something, but they'll tell you, "I see what it says, but I don't really care, because that's not what I believe." We all have to be willing to grow, learn, and accept new understandings that the Lord may give us.

2. Progressive people love truth and a teachable spirit.

Progressive people want to know the truth and won't settle for anything less than the truth. They don't become defensive if an older—or younger—and wiser brother or sister tries to instruct them in some way. By contrast, regressive people are likely to become defensive. They says, "Who are you to teach me? I know what I'm doing, so just leave me alone!"

3. Progressive people have a strong vision, a strong commitment, a strong spirit, and strong relationships with brothers and sisters in Christ.

REPRESSION

Lester Sumrall once said:

It is most interesting to me that God makes every human being full of expression. The moment a baby is born and the doctor spanks the baby, he is looking for expression. If he doesn't get the expression from the child, he pronounces the baby dead. God desires exuberant expression from all of us.

Sometimes when I'm preaching, I might get kind of loud and even shout a little bit. That's because I'm giving expression to the way I feel and the things I want to say. I may even dance or jump a little. That's expression! If I wanted to shout, but whispered instead, that would be repression. If I wanted to jump and dance because the presence of God had made me excited, but instead I stood there like stone, that would be repression. And as I repressed my feelings—my joy and excitement—that joy and excitement would fade away.

Clarence Darrow was a brilliant lawyer who also happened to be an outspoken atheist. You may remember that he defended the theory of evolution and opposed William Jennings Bryan in the Scopes Monkey Trial. Darrow was a great one for giving advice, and one of the bits of advice he gave went something like this: If you're going on a trip by train and you find out that you can sit either by a cold-blooded killer or a fundamental Christian, be sure to choose the cold-blooded killer—for the warmth.

We Christians read that and tend to grimace or think what a blasphemous man Clarence Darrow must have been, but there is some painful truth in that statement. Throughout history, too many God-fearing people thought it was wrong to give expression to the joy and happiness God had given them. They went around with long faces, frowning all the time and looking like they'd been sucking on lemons. They began to quench God's Holy Spirit and became joyless, lifeless, and pathetic. That is the sort of thing repression does to people. Repression may be the outward sign that regression is taking place on the inside. If you don't laugh anymore, maybe you've lost your joy. If you don't dance or shout anymore when God's presence floods the room, it could be because you don't get excited like you used to about the things of God. It can go both ways. Repression can cause regression to begin to take place. But on the other hand, regression can be what causes repression.

Some people have a problem with repression because they were raised in a home where they were never allowed to show their feelings. They might even be the type of people who wait to see what everyone else thinks before they let you know what they think about something. If that's how it is with you, you need to ask God to give you freedom of expression. Maybe you've been hurt. Maybe you've lost a job, a dear friend, or even a spouse. It is OK to mourn and grieve. In fact, Ecclesiastes 3:4 tells us there is a time to weep and mourn. But just as there is a time for mourning, there is a time for getting your life back on track and moving on. Some people allow themselves to get so down, so defeated, and so sad that they become easy prey for demonic influences. A person who is always feeling sad and defeated is a person who is weak and easily overcome, and that's just what demons are looking for.

It's important for us to not only understand repression when we see it in ourselves, but also when we see it in others. Sometimes all we need to do to change things for our sad friends is give them a hug and tell them we appreciate or love them. Maybe all they need is someone to talk to. Just having a friend can make such a difference in people's lives, and it can stop them from falling into demonic oppression and possession.

I think it's funny how people react around certain holidays. Many of us look at the Christmas season as one of great joy. Everywhere you look, you see people who are excited and full of joy and happiness. They absolutely love the Christmas season and everything associated with it. But others are so sad and down-hearted at Christmas. Perhaps it is because their sense of loneliness and hopelessness is only magnified during the holidays. They walk around with lumps in their throats and tears in their eyes. We need to strive to find joy in *everything* God has done for us. But we also need to be the ones who bring God's comfort and joy to those who are struggling with unhappiness—doing everything within our power to lift them out of that state.

God wants exuberant expression from us. He wants us to shout for joy and tell Him in word and deed that we love Him. But if you try to shout "Hallelujah" or give a hearty "Amen" in some churches, they'll tell you to be quiet. They don't want you to feel free to express yourself. That stifling spirit is wrong, harmful, and must be avoided! When I think of expressiveness, I think of heaven. Imagine what it's going to be like with all the angels and all the saved from every nation gathered around the throne of God, singing and praising Him with all our hearts! It's really going to be something! But we ought to be working toward the establishment of a little bit of heaven on earth. We are to worship God here in the same way we're going to worship Him in heaven, and that means giving expression to our most joyful and grateful emotions!

Often, I watch people come into the worship service on Sunday morning, and it's amazing how they change once the service starts. They will be smiling, laughing, and visiting with their friends, but then the worship starts, and they get the longest and weariest expressions! Their children, who were happy and joyful a minute ago, are now forced to be stiff and straight! That's not the way it ought to be. *It's the devil who wants us to be cold and stiff and emotionless, not God!*

I was in a church once that had this big sign up in front that quoted from Habakkuk 2:20: *"The LORD is in his holy temple: let all the earth keep silence before him."* The idea was that people were supposed to come into the building, sit down, and be as quiet as church mice. But as well-intentioned as the people may have been who put that sign up, I think they were dead wrong. One of the things I like to hear in a congregation prior to the start of the worship service is a loud buzz of happy conversation. It's a sign the people really love each other. They're happy to see each other, they're sharing the latest news with one another, and they're talking about all the good things the Lord has done in their lives since they've last seen each other. I think that's great! It's an indication that people are excited about what God has been doing in their lives! Certainly, once the worship service starts, I don't want that buzz of conversation to continue. I want the people to give their full attention to the service, but I want them to do it with the same enthusiasm they had when they were greeting one another earlier.

When we express our excitement and joy regarding what God has done in our lives. Satan and his demons simply cannot stand to be around us. They don't want to hear it. But when we repress those feelings, the demon forces think, *Ah, that's better. I can live with this.* And unfortunately, that's oftentimes what they do.

When I visit some of the holy sites in Israel, I think it's really silly to tiptoe around and whisper in hushed tones, because those are the very places where we need to lift our voices and our hearts in praise to God for what He has done for us! Some people won't like it, but that's OK. God likes it, and He's really the only one who matters!

Too many of today's churches do not give a joyful expression for what God is doing. They do not concentrate on the positive but instead focus most of their attention on the negative. They criticize the preacher or evangelist, because they don't like the way he says things. Never mind the fact that he's bringing healing and deliverance to hundreds or thousands of people.

Someone says, "Did you see that crippled man get out of his wheelchair at last night's service?"

"Oh, sure I did. But I didn't think the sermon was all that great."

Some people worry about the way the evangelist combs his hair or the way he pronounces certain words. They think he's too dramatic, too flamboyant, too slick, or too whatever else they can think of. But none of those things matter. The important thing to think about is: *Are people being ministered to? Are they being saved? Are they being healed and set free from demonic oppression and possession?* If they are, then our response should be to praise God joyfully and perhaps even *noisily* for what He is doing in our midst. God wants us to express, not repress, our feelings.

If there's anything a demon likes better than a blatant sinner, I believe it's a Christian with a negative, critical attitude. He can do more harm with that kind of Christian, because he can sow dissension within the body of Christ. I've seen him use people like that to actually split churches apart. Some people got so disgusted they just walked away and said, "If that's what Christianity is all about, then I don't want anything to do with it." Churches have withered on the vine because of such negativism. They've been completely drained of their evangelistic zeal. They've forgotten and forsaken the calling that was on them, and they might as well nail their doors shut.

Let me give one more example of the way repression can work to damage the human spirit. When a young man and woman fall in love and get married, they constantly tell each other how much they love and care for one another. This is because they're so much in love they really can't help themselves. "I love you" is said often and with great passion. The young man may even tell his bride, "I'll never let a day go by without telling you how much I love you." And he means it when he says it.

But as the years go by and things begin to get in the way, that couple's expression of love for each other comes less and less frequently. They don't say, "I love you" very much, and because they don't, the feelings they once had begin to cool off. The wife says to her husband, "You never tell me you love me anymore!"

And because she says it in an accusing way, her husband snaps back with an "I love you" that really sounds like, "Give me a break! I'm tired today."

Over the years this couple has allowed their feelings for one another to fade away. If they had actually done what they promised they would do—if the man had never let a day go by without telling his wife how much he loved her, and if the wife had done the same, they most likely would have been able to keep their love alive.

If you don't express your feelings, the feelings eventually begin to go away. That happens all too often in our society. No wonder the divorce rate is so high!

Do you love God? Then tell Him! Are you grateful for what He's done in your life? Let Him know. If you repress your feelings, you are bound to grow cold and indifferent, and you will attract unwanted demonic influences. Don't let anything hold you back from expressing your love for God and your joy over what He has done for you.

SUPPRESSION

I define *suppression* as "to squeeze down abnormally." *Suppression* also means "to conceal, as in to suppress information, feelings, and desires." Suppression is closely related to repression, but repression is primarily something we do to ourselves for various reasons. Suppression, on the other hand, is something that comes from outside of us. It is the beginning of demonic inroads being made into a person's life, and it needs to be broken by the power of God.

Suppression can work something like this: Suppose you're in a worship service and you clearly sense that God is talking to you. He has something He wants you to share with the other people who are there, but you just sit there with your mouth shut. You feel like your insides are going to explode, because you want so badly to open your mouth and give this word that God is speaking to you, but you just can't do it! You might even try, but you can't get your mouth to open. It's like one of those dreams you used to have when you were a kid, when a bad guy is coming after you and you try to run, but your legs just won't work. Part of the reason you can't speak this word is because the devil is whispering to you and telling you that you're not really hearing from God or that the other people are going to reject what you have to say,

That is only one form of suppression. It can come in many other ways. Perhaps you have a strong desire to do a particular thing for God, but something is always holding you back. You have a tremendous desire to be used in some type of service for God's kingdom, but when it gets right down to it, it just doesn't happen. I know a man who always wanted to be a missionary to Latin America. When he was in college, he learned to speak Spanish fluently so he could be more effective as a missionary, and he learned everything he could about the Latin American culture. He also went to seminary so he could get a thorough grounding in God's Word. That was over forty years ago, and he has yet to make it to the mission field. By this time in his life, I think it's pretty safe to say he never will. He has done all right in life but has lived in constant disappointment because he has not done the one thing he was certain he was supposed to do, the one thing he really wanted to do.

Why didn't he ever make it to South America? Because of suppression. Something was always squeezing his desires and stopping him before he could follow through. That is what Satan can do to you if you give in to suppression. Suppression cannot be defeated through willpower or by trying harder. It can only be defeated and broken by direct action—by taking authority over it in the name of Jesus and then, in faith, obeying what God has put in your heart to do.

DEPRESSION

Depression is "a psychotic or neurotic condition characterized by an inability to concentrate, insomnia, and feelings of extreme sadness, dejection, and hopelessness." Simply put, *depression* is a broken spirit. A person who is depressed has been pressed down to the point where that person's spirit is crushed. We can all become depressed from time to time. Life in this world can get us down for a variety of reasons. Watching the evening news or reading the morning newspaper is enough to give you a mild dose of depression. However, when we realize God is still on the throne—no matter what happens in the world or in our individual lives, we can keep things in perspective. He is still in charge!

> *And we know that all things work together, for, good to them that love God, to them who are the called according to his purpose.* (Romans 8:28)

For some people, that realization doesn't help. Depression grabs hold of them and will not let go. One chronically depressed person told me he had reached the point where he found no joy in anything he did. All the things that had once given him pleasure were now dead to him. He was only going through the motions, and he felt there was nothing worthwhile in his life, not even his family. You can see why a person like that would be an easy mark for demonic forces that are always on the prowl, looking for someone they can sink their teeth into.

> *Why, my soul, are you downcast? Why so disturbed within me? Put your hope in God, for I will yet praise him, my Savior and my God.* (Psalm 42:5 NIV)

King David knew about depression. But when he became depressed, he chased it away by concentrating on the greatness and goodness of God. He praised God even when he didn't feel like it, and his downcast soul was lifted up when he did.

Legalistic religion can cause depression by bringing people under condemnation.

As we previously discussed regarding religious spirits, those involved in legalistic religion have a form of godliness but deny its power. (See 2 Timothy 3:5.) Religion seeks to control people, and by doing so, takes away their freedom. Legalistic religion says, "You have to do exactly what we tell you to do." In essence, that's saying, "We want you to look to us for guidance in spiritual matters, not God." No wonder people become depressed when they are living in that kind of bondage. We have been saved by the grace of God into a living, intimate relationship with Him. We have not been saved into dead religion. (See Ephesians 2:5.)

Traditions can cause depression.

It is natural to grieve over the death of a loved one, even if you know that loved one has gone on to be with God. Separation is very difficult, even when you're certain there's going to be a reunion someday. But it's possible to take it much too far. For example, some people have traditions that say they must wear black for a year or that if they smile or have fun they're being unfaithful to the deceased. Traditions like that aren't good for anyone. They prolong the grieving process unnaturally and can lead people down into the valley of depression. When a person grieves beyond the natural period of time, the spirit of grief will come in and take control, and the result can be severe, debilitating depression. On the other hand, if you don't allow yourself to grieve, it will come out in some other way in your life, so go ahead and grieve, but realize it is only for a season. Then it is time to put grieving away and get on with your life. (See Ecclesiastes 3:4.)

Depression may be triggered by other forms of loss or trouble.

Getting laid off from your job can bring about depression, as can financial trouble. Not being able to pay your bills and getting harassing phone calls from people you owe is not a source of joy. Having a child rebel against you can bring about depression, as it did with King David. (See 2 Samuel 15–18.) Having a friend turn against you or experiencing the breakup of a romantic relationship can also cause severe depression. It is understandable why some of these events would bring on a state of depression, but it's not understandable why anyone would want to give in to depression and live like that. Yet my own experience tells me that is exactly what happens with some folks.

Some people actually enjoy being depressed, and when you sense that is the case, it's a pretty sure sign of demonic involvement. Some people seem to be professionally depressed. Many stay depressed because it's how they get attention. If that is the case, there's not much anyone can do to help them. I have known people who were in constant need of cheering words and prayer, who wanted every bit of attention I could give them, but none of it did a bit of good. They were depressed and that's how they wanted to stay. For people to gain victory over depression, they have to want to be victorious. We talked in the last chapter about how some people don't want to be delivered from demons because they like having demons in their lives. It's the same thing here. Some people can't be helped because they don't want to be helped. But help is always available for those who want it.

If depression seems to be gaining the upper hand over you, there are several things you can do to shake it off. First, you can pray. Ask God to strengthen you and help you get out from under this thing. Second, praise Him for His greatness and goodness. Isaiah 61:3 tells us to put on *"the garment of praise for the spirit of heaviness,"* and we are instructed throughout the Psalms to praise the Lord, whether we feel like it or not. God inhabits the praises of His people, and depression cannot exist in the presence of the living God. Third, you can take authority over the spirit of depression and break its power through the name of Jesus.

Then he called his twelve disciples together, and gave them power, and authority over all devils, and to cure diseases.

(Luke 9:1)

There are also some natural things you can do to break depression's grip. Sometimes you just need a change of scenery. Get up and leave the room. Go do something different. You may not feel like it, but do it anyway. Depressed people are likely to want to sit in their room and stare at the wall, but that allows depression to feed upon itself. So get up, get dressed, go out, and do something. It might be that a simple change of your environment or routine is the very thing you need to begin to win the battle.

If you are severely depressed, one thing you cannot afford to do is cut yourself off from your brothers and sisters in the Lord. When depression hits, you may want to close yourself off, because you don't feel like being around people who are happy and full of joy. But that's exactly what you need. God knows it's important for us to spend as much time as possible with other believers. We find strength in numbers, and release comes through being surrounded by people of faith—people who will pray with you, minister to you, and love you back from depression. We all need to live up to what the apostle Paul wrote in Galatians 6:2, when he told us to carry each other's burdens. When we really do that, we will always make short work of depression.

The devil would love it if every Christian in the world was depressed. He knows people who are depressed are not energetic or enthusiastic about anything. They are generally lethargic, apathetic, and easily defeated. Depressed people become listless, inactive, and disinterested in what goes on around them, and that means big trouble in the life of a Christian. If Satan could get enough Christians to give in to depression, he would have free reign on this planet. He wouldn't have anyone to oppose him or to bind him, and he would be running roughshod over everyone.

If you are a strong Christian, you can break depression's hold over you all by yourself. But most people need help. If this is you, then by all means ask for help. I've known Christians who were too proud to ask for the help they needed, because they didn't want to appear weak. But it is far better to admit your weakness than to play games while your very life is sapped right out of you. We all need help from time to time, and that's precisely why the Lord gave us to each other! When you sense depression trying to take hold of you, a good response is, "No you don't, in Jesus' name!" Swat that demon back over the fence like you're hitting a tennis ball. Then get involved in what's going on in your church. The saying, "Idle hands are the devil's workshop," is true in a lot of ways. Stay busy in the Lord, and depression won't be able to get its talons into you.

OPPRESSION

Oppression is like depression carried to the nth degree. To *oppress* people means to weigh them down with a load they're not capable of carrying. The dictionary describes it as "keeping one down by severe and unjust use of force or authority." A biblical example is the children of Israel, who were oppressed by Pharaoh. God looked down and had pity on them. He heard their mourning, saw their tears, and sent Moses and Aaron to deliver them.

In the same way, some people today are being oppressed by demons who condemn them, load them up with false guilt, and whisper to them, "You're no good! God couldn't possibly love you." If you are weighed down by your past sins and failures, you are being *oppressed*. I often ask people, "Don't you realize Jesus Christ paid the price for your sins, and they've been washed away by His blood?"

"Oh, yes," they reply. "I know in my head that's true, but I have a hard time getting it down into my heart." Or others say, "But you don't know the things I've done. I want to believe I'm forgiven, but I just can't." If you are struggling with those kinds of feelings, you are a victim of oppression, and you need to deal with it before it deals with you!

One of the ways Christians can fall into oppression is through sickness.

> How God anointed Jesus of Nazareth with the Holy Ghost and with power: who went about doing good, and healing all that were oppressed of the devil; for God was with him.
>
> (Acts 10:38)

During Jesus' earthly ministry, He went about healing those who were oppressed by the devil. Here we see that people who are sick can become oppressed by their illness. Think about how people react when they are told by their doctor that they have cancer. Almost immediately, they will start thinking they are going to die. Even if it was caught in the early stages and is easily treatable, the word *cancer* can nearly destroy a person. People who have serious, long-term illness are often extremely oppressed. They're oppressed because they're worried about the future: *Will I get well? Will I be able to pay my medical bills? What will happen to my family if I don't get well? Am I going to suffer?* With all these thoughts running through their minds, of course they're going to be oppressed.

But there is a solution!

> Come unto Me all ye that labour and are heavy laden, and I will give you rest. Take my yoke upon you, and learn of me; for I am meek and lowly in heart: and ye shall find rest unto your souls, For my yoke is easy, and my burden is light.
>
> (Matthew 11:28–30)

These words of Jesus give the answer for every person who is oppressed by the devil. Some of us try to carry too much on our own shoulders. We worry, we fret, and we run here and there as fast as we can, doing things for the Lord, but we don't let Him help us. We don't come to Him with our burdens and our cares and let Him work through us, so we wind up depressed and oppressed.

In his book, *They Speak With Other Tongues,* John Sherrill tells the story of what happened when he was asked to sing in the church choir. Sherrill, according to his own estimation, didn't have great talent as a singer, but the choir needed some bass voices, so there he was. When he expressed his misgivings, one of the "real" singers gave him some advice, "Just lean into me while we're singing," he said. That's what Sherrill did, and to his surprise he heard his own voice booming forth in clear, deep bass tones. It was almost as if Sherrill's voice was being amplified and carried by the energy coming from the other singer. The application is clear. Lean into the Lord, and you will be surprised at what He is able to do through you. Don't do things for the Lord in your own power. Let Him work through you to accomplish His purposes.

It is said that the famous evangelist, Dwight L. Moody, spent at least one hour in prayer every morning, except when he knew he was facing an extremely busy day. Then he spent two hours in prayer. There was a man who understood the importance of leaning on God. Show me a man or woman who knows how to lean on the Lord, and I'll show you a man or woman who is not oppressed! The servants of God should not strive. They should not be driven by ambition. Their desire should be to obey God in every aspect of life and to rest in God's loving care.

> But seek ye first the kingdom of God, and his righteousness; and all these things shall be added unto you.
>
> (Matthew 6:33)

Oppression is a terrible thing. It can be such a heavy weight hanging over people that it even prevents them from believing the Scriptures. I have prayed for sick people and quickly discovered they were under such a heavy spirit of oppression that they couldn't believe what the Word of God had to say about healing. I would show them how healing was provided for them in the sacrifice of Jesus, and they would say, "Well, I can see the Bible says that, but are you sure that's what it means?"

In a situation like that, the only thing I could do was to take authority over the spirit of oppression. I would tell them, "I break this power over you. I command that this oppression be broken in the name of Jesus. Now spirit man inside of him, stand up! Stand up and realize that Jesus will carry your burdens and heal you of all your diseases." Once that spirit of oppression has been broken, it's much easier for a person to believe and be healed.

Fear can also bring about a spirit of oppression. Some people live in fear. They're afraid they will lose their jobs. They're afraid no one will like them. They're afraid they will go broke. They're afraid they will get sick. They're afraid of the past. They're afraid of the future. I don't care what it is—you name it, and they are afraid of it. If you are living in that kind of fear, you are being oppressed by the devil, and you need to take authority over it! People who are bound by fear have made the mistake of listening to Satan's lies. "You're going to die tomorrow." "Your job is going to be phased out." "Your wife is going to fall out of love with you." And on and on he goes. He is the father of lies, and he never gets tired of telling them.

A person once came to me for prayer who had lived in the world for years and was actively involved in sexual perversion. He said to me, "I'm saved and Spirit-filled now; my life is together, and I'm serving God, but I have a fear that because of the way I lived, AIDS is going to get me."

I said, "Look at me." (I wanted to be sure he was hearing everything I said to him.) Then I told him, "You don't have to worry about AIDS. It's not going to get you."

"Well, how do you know that?"

"Because," I said, "God is in control of your life. He is in control of that situation. If you've come to Jesus, and you've given your life to God, and you've asked Him to cleanse you, He'll also cleanse your body from any type of thing that would cause that disease to get you. Believe God and live! Don't let these lies from Satan control your life!"

That's another reason people are oppressed. They come to Jesus and find forgiveness and freedom from their past sins, but Satan keeps whispering to them. "You're not really free. You're still going to suffer the consequences of all those things you've done in the past." It's just not true. If Jesus has set you free, you are free indeed.

When I am ministering to someone who is bothered by a spirit of oppression. I really try to knock it out of them. I make them look at me and listen to me. Sometimes I make them repeat after me words of power and release, and when they do, I make them repeat it with authority. I want them to hear themselves, and I want them to say it so forcefully that they can't help but believe it. Oppression can be deadly, but it is no match for the power of God.

OBSESSION

Obsession is not always bad. Some people are obsessed with the things of God, and that's a good thing. If you're so obsessed with things of the Spirit that some people call you "a fool for Christ," you can feel very good about the life you're living. But there is an evil form of obsession as well, and it can be a terrible and cruel taskmaster. A person who is obsessed is one who is preoccupied with an idea, feeling, or emotion that cannot be broken by natural means. It is a persistent, inescapable, compulsive preoccupation.

For example, you may have heard about the young woman who was obsessed with the idea that she was David Letterman's wife. Letterman himself said he had never met the woman, but she was totally obsessed with him. She broke into his house and did all sorts of things a normal person wouldn't do because of that obsession. She was arrested, but that did not break the hold this obsession had over her. She was placed in jail, but that did not break it. She was publicly ridiculed and embarrassed, but that did not break her obsession or change her behavior. Admittedly, that's an unusual case. But it's an example of what obsession can do to a person. Usually, the obsessions people develop are more acceptable in the eyes of the world. In other words, they don't cause headlines and hold people up to public ridicule, but they can be just as dangerous, just as deadly to the human spirit, and just as difficult to overcome.

Many people become obsessed with pornography, sex, or sexual perversion. Some become obsessed with the occult or New Age teachings. Young people may become obsessed with certain types of music. It's possible to be obsessed with money. Whatever you can think of, it's possible for someone to be obsessed with it. It can start out innocently enough. A Christian businessman is on a trip and a long way from home. After a long day of meetings, he retires to his hotel room, turns on the television, and begins flipping through the channels. There, on one of the channels, is a sexually explicit movie. As soon as he sees what it is, he changes the channel, but he can't get it out of his mind, and soon he flips back to it, thinking, *It won't hurt me to see what this is all about. After all,* he tells himself, *I'm just curious—it's not like I'm really interested.* So he sits there and watches the movie until it's over, and by the time it's over, he's hooked. He tries to turn away, but he can't.

That's how quickly an obsession can take control of you. You have to always be on guard against Satan's tricks. Don't think you're so strong you would never fall into temptation. Jesus instructed us to pray, *"Lead us not into temptation"* (Matthew 6:13). He did not tell us to say, "Lead us into a temptation or two so we can resist it and thereby show You how strong we are." Satan is doing his best to hit you where you are weakest, so pray you will be able to avoid what he is throwing at you. Don't listen to what he wants to say to you. Don't look at what he wants you to see. He wants to hook you and reel you in like a fish.

When you are obsessed with something, you get in deeper and deeper into more blatant types of sin. When people are obsessed with some type of sinful behavior, they have opened themselves up to invasion by an evil spirit related to that desire. In the case of obsession, your desires become the demon's desires, and a devil is always obsessed with some sin or another. For example, people who are troubled by a lying spirit will not be able to tell the truth. They are not lying to protect themselves or to avoid telling the truth about some painful issue. They are simply lying because that's all they can do. Ask them what day it is, and they may tell you it is Tuesday even though they know it is Monday. Ask them for directions, and they will send you in the opposite direction from the way you really need to go. They are obsessed with lying. Similarly, people who are troubled by a sex devil just can't think about anything else. It is all they can think about or talk about—all they live for.

You can see how terrible it is to be obsessed. People who are victims of one of these devils may try to shake it off at first. They tell themselves they are going to change, but they are totally powerless on their own, and those devilish fangs sink deeper and deeper into their souls. Soon they reach the point where they don't see anything wrong with their behavior. They have lost the understanding of what is right and what is wrong. Unless the obsession is broken through God's divine power, such people are doomed.

Here are several ways an obsession can begin.

Obsession can begin when you believe a lie.

"It won't hurt me to see just one X-rated movie."

"I don't see anything wrong with having a few drinks."

"I'm not doing anything wrong—just flirting a little bit with my secretary."

One lie can lead to another. One improper step can be followed by another, until you have strayed far from the proper path. Don't be taken in by any of the devil's lies. Instead, look to the Holy Spirit to guide you in every situation.

Obsession can begin when you give in to jealousy.

A husband decides his wife is not to be trusted. She really hasn't done anything wrong, but he has these nagging suspicions that just won't go away. He begins to question her in accusing tones about everything she does. "Where did you go today? What did you do? Who did you see?" Soon two lives have all but been destroyed by the husband's obsessive jealously. Jealousy is one of the devil's favorite tools. He uses it to cause strife among human beings. The "green-eyed monster" can break up marriages, family relationships, friendships, businesses, and churches. Be careful not to give in to jealousy. It can destroy you!

Hatred can open the door to obsession.

As Christians, we're not to hate anyone. Instead, Jesus told us we are to love our enemies. (See Matthew 5:44.) I don't care what people have done or how unlovable they might be, we are to love them. However Christians may find themselves intensely disliking other people. If you find that happening to you, begin to pray for that person. Ask God to bless that person. Ask God to help you see things from that person's point of view. Don't give in to the demons that want your heart to be full of hate.

Some people have gotten into real trouble, not because they have hated others but because they have assumed others didn't like them. They think they are being excluded from things. They look for ways they have been slighted. They turn an innocent remark into a terrible insult. When that begins to happen, you can be sure demons are whispering their lies: "No one likes you. They're all mean to you. You need to get even with them." What those devils really want is to isolate and conquer you. Don't let it happen!

Obsession can come through being involved in some type of sin.

This means indulging in something you know is wrong to the point where your willpower is totally gone. It's like what happens to a drug addict. When they first begin taking drugs, they tell themselves they only do it because it makes them feel good, and they can stop anytime they want to. But as time goes on, they begin to realize that isn't really true. They get to the point where they couldn't stop if their life depended on it—and sometimes it does. One major league baseball player has been arrested and charged with possession of cocaine not once, not twice, not three times, but *seven* times. He lost his marriage, and he very nearly lost his career. He was banned from baseball for life and then reinstated. He had warning after warning and has promised to get his life straightened out. But until now, he keeps going back to the drug. That's what can happen when a person begins to transgress God's laws. An old Chinese proverb says, "A journey of 1,000 miles begins with one step." That is true of any journey, including the journey into the bondage of obsession. If you want to maintain your freedom, don't ever take that first small step away from what you know is right.

POSSESSION

The seventh and last step on the road to demonic possession is possession itself. This is the final step in which the devil captures the immortal soul. Demon-possessed people live all over the world, but most people who are bothered by devils are in one of the six other categories we've discussed. To be demon-possessed means to be under absolute and total control of the devil. Your willpower is owned by the spirit that lives in you. In some of the other cases we have discussed, demons may have been involved in the mind and the body, but not in the spirit. People who are possessed have a demon or demons living within their spirits. A person can become possessed by failing to resist demonic attacks. For instance, suppose a lying spirit was attacking you. If you don't resist it through the name and the blood of Jesus, that spirit would continue to work on you, night and day, until it was finally able to gain entrance into your spirit.

If you are a born-again, Spirit-filled Christian and you come into close proximity with someone who is demon-possessed, that person will react to you in some way. It may be major or minor. For example, they may speak with a voice that is not human or with one that is not their natural voice. A grown man may speak with the voice of a little boy, or a woman may speak with a deep man's voice. They may not even speak at all, but may bark like a dog or growl like some other animal. Sometimes their voices will change as they're talking to you—going from very high pitched to very low-pitched and back again in a matter of minutes.

I saw one case where the possessed person's tongue came out of her mouth like a snake and made a clicking sound. It wasn't hard to tell that this was in the hands of a demonic entity.

Sometimes you can even spot demon possession by the way people carry themselves. There's something about the way they walk, the way they hold their heads and move their arms. There's something sinister about their body movements. I'm not saying you should be suspicious of anyone whose moves are a little different from normal, but certain characteristics can indicate demonic involvement in someone's life.

Once a couple came to me and asked if I could help their ten-year-old little boy. They explained that he would go into fits of terrible rage and anger, running through the house and destroying everything he could. He smashed mirrors, kicked lamps onto the floor, and threw furniture against the walls. He would be sitting there nice and sweet one minute, and the next minute he was acting like a raving-mad lunatic. These poor parents had taken their son to doctors and psychiatrists in an effort to help him, but nothing worked. Of course it hadn't worked! The little boy was possessed by a demon, and once it was cast out of him, he was fine.

This is a common situation. I am convinced America's mental institutions are full of people who are not mentally ill at all, but possessed by demons. They don't need years and years of expensive psychiatric therapy. They need someone to cast those demons out of them in the power and authority of Jesus! That's what you will see in church services when the Spirit of God really begins to move. Just as the anointing of the Holy Spirit enters the room, the devils will begin to scream and shout and do their best to disrupt things. When that happens, you need to move forward in Jesus' authority. Cast out those demons that are causing such trouble, and then get on with the celebration of God's presence and power!

To be possessed by an evil spirit is a terrible thing—the worst sort of bondage imaginable. In our world today, thousands upon thousands of people are trapped. They need to be set free, and they can be set free if Christians will move forward in the power and authority of God. I've said it before, but I need to say it again. There isn't a demon in the universe that can stand against the power of

God. In fact, all the demons in the universe put together, including Satan himself, couldn't stand against the power of God. If you are living in the power of God, you have nothing at all to fear from demons—and they have *everything* to fear from you!

CHAPTER 7

MOVING FORWARD IN THE POWER OF GOD

In this book, we've learned quite a bit about demons. We know where they come from. We've talked about their leader, Lucifer, who is now called Satan, and how he fell from heaven. We have learned that demons are the ones responsible for haunted houses and ghostly sightings and that they are involved in many other occult activities and New Age practices. We have discovered how Jesus dealt with demons and that the early church had to deal with demons, too. We also learned that demons can gain entrance into the human spirit. That leaves one very important matter to be discussed: *How you can take authority over Satan and his armies from hell.*

When I look out my window on a clear, autumn evening, I can see the lights of my neighborhood filtering through the trees. If it is a clear night, I see the beautiful moon in the western sky. I often hear the droning of an airplane engine and see the lights blinking on and off as it passes overhead. In my neighborhood, this is a normal night, and anyone who didn't know better would say all is right with the world. Things are just the way they're supposed to be. But that's not true. A war is raging all around us. On a calm, clear night, it doesn't seem like a war is in progress, but nevertheless, light and dark are warring for control of every human being on this planet.

Because of that, in this chapter, I will share eight principles for how you can operate in the power of Jesus Christ when faced with demonic activity.

1. Know you are in a real war.

We have all been summoned to fight in this war. If you belong to Jesus, you are a soldier. You need to take this war—and your part in it—very seriously. You need to be trained so you not only recognize the enemy but are equipped to defeat him in hand-to-hand combat. Make no mistake about it—if you are ready and willing to be used, there will be plenty of hand-to-hand combat. After all, every Christian has been given a ministry of deliverance. We have all been called into this battle against the powers of darkness.

> *And he said unto them. Go ye into all the world, and preach the gospel to every creature. He that believeth and is baptized shall be saved; but he that believeth not shall be damned. And these signs shall follow them that believe. In my name shall they cast out devils, they shall speak with new tongues. They shall take up serpents, and if they drink any deadly thing, it shall not hurt them; they shall lay hands on the sick, and they shall recover.* (Mark 16:15–18)

This is known as the Great Commission. Take a closer look at verse 17, which says, *"In my name shall they cast out devils."* Who is Jesus talking about here? He is talking about all who believe in Him. Do you believe in Jesus? Have you surrendered your life to Him? Is He your Lord and Savior? If so, this applies to you, and you should be driving out demons in His name.

I don't know how old you are. You may be twelve or you may be 102; it really doesn't matter, because you are never too young or too old to be a soldier in the war that rages throughout the entire cosmos. Some churches don't talk about deliverance, because they are embarrassed by the subject. Some don't talk about it, because they're flat-out afraid of devils. I assure you that any church that is embarrassed or ashamed of deliverance or afraid of devils definitely needs deliverance.

Don't be afraid. God has given you His power, but it's up to you to use it. You should use it wherever and whenever it's needed! Always remember that demons fear you, because you belong to Jesus. The power of God is flowing through you, and that means no demon can withstand you.

2. Remember who you are in Jesus.

When you confront demons, they may tell you they don't have to listen to you. They'll say you are weak, and they may remind you that you are a sinner. However, they do have to listen to you, because you belong to Jesus, and you operate in His power and authority. Yes, it may be true that you are a weak human being and that you sin. But you have been justified and sanctified by the blood of Jesus. When God looks at you, He does not see even the slightest smudge of sinful behavior. He sees only the righteousness that was given to you by His only begotten Son!

> *For, he hath made him to be sin for, us, who knew no sin; that we might be made the righteousness of God in him.*
>
> (2 Corinthians 5:21)

When Jesus ascended into heaven, He gave us His name, which represents His victory, His capacity, and His ability to deal with any situation—including a confrontation with the worst demons hell has produced. Use the name of Jesus. Demons don't want to hear it, because it reminds them they are defeated and doomed. It is the only name that gives you authority over all the powers of hell. Sometimes the demons will try to bargain with you. They will try to convince you they don't really mean any harm and they're not really demons. They will do all sorts of things to trick you into leaving them alone. Don't listen. Don't be taken in. Cast them out by the authority of Jesus' name.

They will try to break your concentration and maybe even scare you a little bit by shocking you so you'll back off and leave them alone. You may encounter a demon-possessed person who is talking in a normal human voice, and the next thing you know, that person is roaring like a lion or barking like a dog. Or the demon may cause its victim's body to go into strange contortions. It may be like the movie, *The Exorcist*, where the demon-possessed girl kept vomiting up a substance that looked remarkably like pea soup! Whatever the demon may do, don't let it dissuade you from the task at hand. Remember who you are in Jesus, and cast that demon out.

Do you know who you are? You are an ambassador of the King of kings. (See 2 Corinthians 5:20.) You are a new creature in Christ. (See 2 Corinthians 5:17.) You are an ambassador of the New Jerusalem. You are the one God has sent to deliver this person from the grip of Satan. You are the one who has power over all the works of the devil. Do you understand this? Do you believe it is absolutely true? The power that created everything around you is resident within you.

Do you see yourself as just a frail little girl? You are a mighty warrior in Christ! Do you consider yourself to be a feeble old man? You, too, are a mighty warrior in Christ! I don't care if you are blind, are confined to a wheelchair, or have any other physical frailty or handicap; in Christ you are a warrior and will always be victorious over the forces of evil, just as the shepherd boy David was victorious over the mighty giant Goliath. (See 1 Samuel 17:4–58.)

You must face devils from your position and your authority. Don't come against them indecisively, trying to somehow tiptoe around them. You must face them as if you were a boxer, staring at your opponent across the other side of the ring. Dogs can sense it when a human is afraid of them. It's the same with demons. If they look at you and see no fear in you, they will be afraid and know they are defeated.

3. Pray in tongues.

> *Therefore put on the full armour of God, so that when the day of evil comes, you may be able to stand your ground, and after you have done everything, to stand....And pray in the Spirit on all occasions with all kinds of prayers and requests. With this in mind, be alert and always keep on praying for the Lord's people.* (Ephesians 6:13, 18 NIV)

Praying in tongues while you are casting out a demon helps to keep you alert and involved in the battle, so you are quickly aware when the demons try to trick you. Perhaps you are reading this, and you don't pray in tongues. If that's the case, it means you have not been baptized in the Holy Spirit, and that's something you should seek. If you have not experienced the baptism in the Holy Spirit, you are not Spirit-filled and are not operating in the full capacity of spiritual strength God has available to you. Yes, you can be saved and not be baptized in the Holy Spirit. You can be living for Jesus and not be baptized in the Holy Spirit, but you are missing something important. Read the book of Acts to find out what the Bible has to say about being filled with the Holy Spirit. Also, many good books have been written on this subject, and I strongly urge you to do some serious reading and praying.

Whenever I cast out demons, I pray in English and also in tongues. As I mentioned, praying in tongues helps keep me extra alert as to what is going on, and that's important. The devil never runs out of tricks, and neither do his foot soldiers. For example, the demons may try to convince you they have left their victim when they really haven't left at all. If I have been praying in tongues, I can discern this and continue ordering them to leave until they're really gone.

Another thing that happens is that one or two demons, or perhaps even more, will actually be cast out of someone, but they will leave more and stronger demons behind. Remember that a single human being may be the home of many demons. You're making a tragic mistake if you quit before the job is done—before the strongman inside a person's spirit has been bound and cast out. But if you're praying in tongues and are tuned in to the direction of the Holy Spirit, you'll know when the battle has been won. You will not be fooled.

4. Use the gifts of the Holy Spirit.

Now to each one the manifestation of the Spirit is given for the common good. To one there is given through the Spirit the message of wisdom, to another the message of knowledge by means of the same Spirit, to another faith by the same Spirit, to another gifts of healing by that one Spirit, to another miraculous powers, to another prophecy, to another distinguishing between spirits, to another speaking in different kinds of tongues, and to still another the interpretation of tongues. All these are the work of one and the same Spirit, and he distributes them to each one, just as he determines.

(1 Corinthians 12:7–11 NIV)

This cannot apply to you if you have not experienced the baptism in the Holy Spirit. If that is the case with you, you are trying to fight demons without crucial weapons.

Many times when I have been casting out a demon, the Holy Spirit has given me a word of knowledge or a word of wisdom. I have been able to say, "Look, you've had this particular problem and that's what opened you up to demonic influences." The Lord may reveal to me that this person has a problem with unforgiveness or unconfessed sin. Sometimes I have to tell a person, "If you don't forgive this is person, I can't cast this demon out," or, "If you don't confess this sin to the Lord, I can't get rid of this thing."

It has been supernaturally revealed to me on more then one occasion that a person I was praying for had been opened up to demons as a result of being abused as a child. The Holy Spirit has also allowed me to see when a lying spirit was given entrance into a person's spirit because abusive parents made that person afraid to tell the truth about things as a child. You can see how valuable that information is with regard to bringing total healing and freedom into that person's life. I'm always happy when it is revealed to me how and why a demon was able to gain entrance into someone's life. It's great to be able to clear the demons out of a person's life, and it's wonderful to be able to help that person realize what changes need to be made—with the Lord's help—in order to prevent the return of those demons. If the gifts of the Spirit are working in you, you'll know what to do in every situation. The same is true if you are yielded to God and operating in the power and direction of the Holy Spirit.

Sometimes an anointing will come upon you to deal with certain types of evil spirits or certain types of situations. It doesn't mean you can't deal with anything the devil throws at you; it just means God has given you a special strength to deal with certain needs at that moment. I have found that such an anointing may not last all that long, so I want to make the most of it while I have it. God may give me, for a brief period, a special anointing to deal with spirits that are linked to sexual perversion. If that's the case, I want to act on that instead of spending my time casting out lying spirits or spirits tied to things like unconfessed sin. Someone may say, "But aren't the people who are afflicted by those other kinds of demons just as important as those who are troubled by spirits of sexual perversion?" Of course they are! But at this particular point in time, I have been given a special anointing to cast out those sex devils, and I must move in that anointing.

In my meetings, you will sometimes see me call for helpers to come and deal with certain types of demons. When I do, it's because I realize a special type of anointing has been placed on me, and I don't want to step outside of that anointing to deal with other types of problems. I know God well enough that I'm convinced He wouldn't give anyone a special anointing if there wasn't an urgent need for it. God is very economical, and He always does the thing that will do the most good for the most people. That's why it is so very important to follow His leading.

5. Ask them if they want to be free.

You may think, *Who wouldn't want to be set free?* But it is true—some people don't want to be free, and even though it's possible to cast devils out of them, you may be wasting your time. Those devils will come right back and invade that person again, because they know they're wanted. Of course, in some instances, people can't tell you they want to be set free, because the demons within them won't let them tell you. At times you just have to take authority, no matter what the person might say.

As a basic rule, when I find out people have demons because they invited them in, and they don't really want to be rid of them, I just leave them alone. Sometimes I'll ask questions like, "Do you want to live this perverted life? Do you really want this lifestyle?"

It could be that no one has ever asked a question like that before. Sometimes they will respond with puzzlement: "What do you mean?"

Then I have to get forceful, "I mean, do you want to live in this state of mental derangement for the rest of your life, or do you want to be free and live a good life?"

If the answer is, "I want to be free," I will ask, "Do you really mean that?" If they say they do, and I sense they're telling the truth, I will move right into deliverance—taking authority in the name of Jesus and casting that demon out.

6. Have faith in the name of Jesus.

The name of Jesus contains tremendous power, but that power is activated only by faith in His name. Remember the story of the Jewish exorcists who tried to cast out demons *"in the name of Jesus whom Paul preaches"*? Instead of obeying the command to come out of their victim, the demons reacted violently, and the exorcists were fortunate to escape with their lives! (See Acts 19:15.) They had no right to use the name of Jesus, because they didn't believe in Him or His name. Therefore, it had no power for them.

You must believe wholeheartedly in Jesus before you can use His name to cast out demons. Are you living for Him? Do you have a regular time to commune with Him daily? Do you study and meditate upon the Word of God so much that it is down inside of you and you can draw upon it when you need it? Do you understand and believe in the power of the Word of God? If you don't have faith that what the Bible says is true, you can quote it to demons all day long, and they'll just stay in there and yawn. They won't care. If it doesn't have any meaning to you, it won't have any meaning to them when you try to use it.

When you say, "In the name of Jesus, come out of that person," you have to understand that the name you're using is the name above all names. It is the name that will cause every living creature to bow in complete reverence and worship. (See Philippians 2:10–11.) The blessed, holy, wonderful name of Jesus! When you use the name of Jesus, it is like a bomb exploding and knocking evil out of the way.

7. Don't be nervous.

I understand you're bound to be a bit nervous the first time you step forward in faith to cast out devils. But ask God to help you move out in boldness and faith and to take away the nervousness you feel. He will do it. It is so important that you learn to stay as peaceful as possible, concentrating on the glory and power of Jesus Christ. I have had experiences in which it seemed like a fullscale battle was raging all around me. People were crawling around on the floor and slithering like snakes; others were growling and barking or whining and crying. Yet in the middle of it, I felt a great peacefulness. That is the peace that passes human understanding, and it is available to you as a child of God.

It's not always the demons who make you nervous. Sometimes you may be surprised by the person you're praying for. I have seen prayer lines where respected community and church leaders have come forward, and it quickly becomes apparent they have deep-rooted demonic involvement in their lives. The natural tendency would be to say, "Oh, I can't believe you are troubled by demons!" Don't worry about it. Just cast that demon out, and then go on with your life. *Always remember that deliverance has not been given so you can judge people. Deliverance has been given so you can set people free.* Often people who are respected in a community or church don't get the help they need because they are embarrassed. Pride is what keeps them bound. So when you find yourself ministering deliverance to someone you have looked up to and respected, don't be nervous, and don't let it diminish the way you feel about that person. Just get that person free and praise God that He is using you as a conduit for His power.

That brings me to another very important point. Don't talk about the experience after it's over. It's true that immediately afterward, you may have to talk to the people who were delivered and explain what has happened just to make sure they follow it and realize they've been set free by the power of Jesus. But once you've done that, let it go and forget about it. With the right attitude, it can be a good idea to occasionally check up on people who has been set free. Call them on the phone or drop by and ask how they're doing. Have they experienced any problems? Have there been any more demonic attacks? If so, ask them to pray with you and ask the Lord to continue to protect and minister to them. Remind the devil, together, that you have cast him out, and he has no authority over them. Then remind people how to take authority over the forces of evil when they attack. Remind them they don't have to listen to them, and if they resist demons in the name of Jesus, they will flee.

Always remember that your time together and your conversation is confidential. It should remain between the two of you, so don't share it with anyone else. To be blunt about it, it is nobody else's business! Don't go around the church telling everyone you know that you just cast a demon out of so-and-so. And don't walk up to so-and-so every time you see him or her after that and say, "Remember that time I cast the demon out of you?" No good purpose is served by that kind of behavior. What has happened has happened, so let it go and move on.

It is possible to flow in the Spirit to the point that you may not even remember afterward who you were dealing with. People have come up to me and said, "Remember me? I'm the one you cast that demon out of last week?"

And I have to apologize and say, "No, I'm sorry, but I really don't remember you at all."

I don't want to hurt anyone's feelings, but when I'm in a large service and numbers of people are coming forward for healing or deliverance, I'm operating in the power of the Spirit. The Holy Spirit is working through me to the point that I sometimes won't remember things I've said or done, even moments after I've said or done them!

8. There is power in the laying on of hands.

Don't be afraid to put your hands on the demon-possessed person. When the power of God is flowing through you, it will flow right out of your hands into the body of the person you're ministering to. Read through the book of Acts, and you'll find the Holy Spirit was often given by the laying on of the apostles' hands. There is a spiritual principle at work here, so use it.

When you have your hands on the body of a victim of possession, you may feel the evil spirit moving in that person's body. I have had my hands on someone's stomach and have felt the demon moving upward, through the chest, the throat, and finally out the mouth. A demonic knot can actually be felt moving through the body on its way out. Often, people will begin to choke as the demon moves through the throat. I've had people start to cry and panic, "I can't breathe! I'm choking! I'm going to die!"

Whenever that happens, I tell them to calm down because the demon is in the process of leaving the body, and they are not going to die. Instead, they are going to live in a joyous freedom they have not known before.

Practice the laying on of hands. If you are living for God your hands belong to Him, and He wants to let His power flow through them.

At the start of this chapter, I told you a war is raging in the universe. It is absolutely true. But I want you to understand that the outcome has already been decided. It's like the old preacher said, "I've looked in the back of the book, and guess what? We win!" But even though the devil doesn't have any chance of being victorious, he is still intent on causing as many casualties as he possibly can. The outcome of the war has been determined, but vicious and bloody fighting continues. Satan continues his indiscriminate attacks on people of all ages, races, and lifestyles. We must stop him and his armies. We must fight back. God has given us absolute power over the forces of darkness, and He commands us to advance against the enemy.

The time has come to go forth and conquer in the mighty name of Jesus!

ABOUT THE AUTHOR

Roberts Liardon is an author, public speaker, spiritual leader, church historian, and humanitarian. He was called into the ministry at a very young age, preaching his first public sermon at the age of thirteen and lecturing in Christian colleges and universities at age fifteen.

At sixteen, Roberts launched a radio program, and at seventeen, he wrote his first book, *I Saw Heaven*, which sold 1.5 million copies. His next book and video series, *God's Generals*, established Roberts as a leading Protestant church historian, and both books brought him international attention.

In his mid-twenties, Roberts built one of the fastest growing churches in the US, and established his first accredited Bible college. From this ministry, he founded more than forty churches, built five international Bible colleges, and assisted the poor and needy in his community, throughout America, and around the globe. Recently, Roberts launched a new TV show called *God's Generals with Roberts Liardon*, which currently airs in more than two hundred nations.

Roberts had the privilege of being mentored by Oral Roberts and Lester Sumrall, and now he is under the covering of both Dr. Che Ahn of Harvest International Ministry and Pastor Colin Dye of Kensington Temple, London, England. As a recognized church historian specializing in the Pentecostal and charismatic movements, he is much in demand as a speaker, writer, and mentor. His voice speaks to a current generation of believers who want to draw closer to the heart and mind of God and impact their communities and the nations of the world through the gospel of Jesus Christ.

You may contact Dr. Liardon at:

Roberts Liardon Ministries
www.robertsliardon.com
Facebook: Roberts Liardon Official
Twitter: Roberts Liardon

U.S. Office:
Roberts Liardon Ministries
P.O. Box 2989, Sarasota
FL 34230
E-mail: Admin@robertsliardon.org

UK and Europe Office:
Roberts Liardon Ministries
UK, 22 Notting Hill Gate, Suite 125
London W11 3JE, UK
E-mail: Admin@robertsliardon.org